Approaching Christian Scripture Faithfully

Twenty Attempts

Ed Gallagher

CYPRESS

Catalog in Publication

Gallagher, Ed (Edmon Louis), 1979-
Approaching Christian scriptures faithfully : twenty attempts/ Ed
Gallagher
p. cm.
Includes scripture index.
1. Bible–Criticism, interpretation, etc. I. Author. II. Title.
220.6 DDC21
ISBN: 978-1-956811-41-4 (pbk.) ; 978-1-956811-42-1 (ebook).
LCCN: 2023935643

Cover designed by Brad McKinnon and Brittany Vander Maas.

For more information:

Cypress Publications

PO Box HCU

3625 Helton Drive

Florence, AL 35630

www.hcu.edu/publications

For my sister,
Elaine Brown,
a model of faith

Contents

Preface   vii

Section 1   1
The Old Testament

1. A Prostitute's Wish   2
Approaching 1 Kings 3

2. A Still Small Voice   14
Approaching 1 Kings 19

3. A Time for Defiance   34
Approaching Esther 3

4. The Challenge of Love   48
Approaching Hosea

5. Does Amos Condemn All Sacrifice?   57
Approaching Amos 5

Section 2   66
The New Testament

6. The Bible Is Our Blueprint   67
Approaching Luke 4:1–13

7. God Is Our Foundation   76
Approaching Matthew 7:24–27 // Luke 6:46–49

8. Using Your Talents   85
Approaching Matthew 25:14–30

9. Faith at the Cross   92
Approaching Luke 23:42

10. A Sickness Not Unto Death   100
Approaching John 11

11. Not Under the Law   113
Approaching Galatians 5:18

12. The Bible on Slavery   122
Approaching Ephesians 6:4–9

13. On Faith   136
Approaching Hebrews 11:1

Section 3   145
The Church

14. Why the Church?   146
15. The Kingdom of God   154
16. The Israel of God   161
17. Corporate Worship as Spiritual Discipline   169
18. A Worshiping Community on a Mandated
    Break   185

Section 4   212
Miscellaneous

19. What Is a Canon?   213
20. My Friend Doesn't Believe in God   225
    An Address to Teenagers

Bibliography   231

Scripture Index   239

Credits   254

Also by Ed Gallagher   256

Heritage Christian University Press   258

Preface

Scripture, rich with meaning, rewards constant study as much as it resists definitive explication. The Mishnah from around AD 200 reports the comment of a Rabbi named Ben Bag-Bag that captures this aspect of Scripture: "Turn it every which way, for everything is in it; and meditate on it; and grow old and worn with it; and never abandon it—for there is no lot better than this."[1] This saying helpfully captures the wealth of meanings inherent in Scripture.

This positive evaluation of Scripture's multilayered interpretive potential may sound very postmodern—though, as Ben Bag-Bag reminds us, it's also very premodern. Not only the Rabbis but also early Christians—or, actually, all readers of Scripture up until the last few hundred years—assumed that any given passage of Scripture could give way to multiple meanings, that there was no single meaning intended by the divine author but potentially many.[2] And any reader committed to learning biblical interpretation from the New Testament is forced to grapple with the potential of varied meanings in a biblical passage; otherwise, what can we do with Matthew's interpretation of Hosea 11:1 (Matt 2:15)? Or Paul's assertion that the rock providing water to the Israelites in the wilderness (cf. Exod 17:6; Num 20:7–11) was actually a single rock that traveled with the Israelites, "and the rock was Christ" (1 Cor 10:4)?[3] Or many other examples in which the New Testament author uses Scripture in a way that is hardly straightforward? Christians are encouraged by our Scripture to read Scripture in multiple ways.[4] And we are going to have to pay careful attention to what we read, and be open to new possibilities, if we're to have any chance of keeping up with Paul and John and the other authors of the New Testament.

The encouragement to come back again to Scripture, to examine it anew, to try to see things in it that we haven't seen before, is a traditional point of emphasis for the American Restoration Movement. This movement, of which I am a descendent, received energy and direction from two men in particular in the first half of the nineteenth century: Barton W. Stone (d. 1844) and Alexander Campbell (d. 1866), so much so that some modern scholars name the movement after these men (the Stone-Campbell Movement).[5] The Restoration Movement began with an emphasis on Scripture.[6] Whatever the goal originally was—whether it was the restoration of the primitive church, or the unity of all believers, or ushering in the millennium—the movement certainly had to do with biblical interpretation. To confirm this point, simply pick up a copy of Stone's brief document *The Last Will and Testament of the Springfield Presbytery* (1804) or the much longer *Declaration and Address* (1809) of Thomas Campbell (father of Alexander). Readers of these documents cannot but be impressed with the constant call to examine the Scriptures again.

The early days of the Restoration Movement were taken up mostly with trying to determine what God wants people to do—either how (the process by which) people should become Christians as revealed in the New Testament (i.e., the plan of salvation) or how Christians should conduct themselves in church (especially with regard to worship). To determine these points, it was decided that the focus of study should not be the Old Testament (which doesn't talk about Christians at all) or even the Gospels (which hardly mention the word "church"), but rather the Acts of the Apostles and the apostolic epistles. While the entire Bible was considered authoritative, it was pointed out, correctly, that the entire Bible does not speak to the issues about how to become a Christian or what to do in church. That was the special province of Acts and the epistles, and so those sections of Scripture became the particular objects of study for the movement. (This focus can be seen already in the "Sermon on the Law," preached by Alexander Campbell in 1816.)[7] Again, the emphasis was on what people should do. This kind of emphasis did not lend itself to the pursuit of multiple possible meanings, but rather to isolating the most appropriate course of action, the one Christian virtue, taught by a biblical text. In my opinion, this pursuit has produced helpful results and has pushed readers to dig further into Scripture.

And what we find when we look at Scripture is that Scripture is not primarily about me at all. From Genesis to Revelation, the Bible is about God. Different parts of Scripture reveal to us different aspects about our God, different elements of his character, different ways in which he relates to us. It is legitimate to ask what God wants from us—and even more specifically, how we should become Christians, and what Christian worship should entail. And to answer those questions, it makes sense to focus our energies on the parts of the Bible designed to address those issues. It might even make sense to talk about the Bible as a "blueprint" for our lives, as people have often done, including me. (You'll find a chapter in this book exploring that concept.) But if we're turning our gaze away from ourselves and toward our God—the chief topic of every part of Scripture—then our reading must also expand beyond the familiar confines of the New Testament and encompass the entire Christian Bible. And if our question is not about what we should do but rather is about what God wants us to know about Himself and about the nature of humanity and about sin and about love and about ethics and about all kinds of other things, then it becomes more worthwhile to pursue the multiple layers of meaning built into the text of Scripture.

And that's part of the reason I insist on calling what I'm doing here "attempts" at approaching Christian Scripture faithfully. Another reason for insisting on that word, "attempts," is that the Bible can be hard to understand. The gospel is easy to understand; the Bible rarely is. (See further reflections on this idea in chapter 17.) I have no illusions that I am offering the definitive interpretation of a Scriptural passage; in fact, I would dispute the very notion. I continue to hope that when I later turn to some of the very same passages that serve as the focus of some of the studies collected here, I will be able to find things that so far elude me. Probably you have heard, as I have, similar comments in Bible class all your life, comments like: "you can never fathom the depth of Scripture; there's always more to find." That is exactly what I am encouraging and attempting here. I could have called this collection, *Practicing Biblical Inter-*

pretation, with the double meaning of the word "practice" nicely capturing not only the idea of "attempt" but even the concept of multiple meanings for those who are willing to "turn it," as Ben Bag-Bag advises.

I should say something about the origins of these chapters. Almost all of these essays have been published before, mostly by Heritage Christian University Press in various books, but also by a few other presses. The original publication data is given at the start of each chapter. As you can see from the Table of Contents, most of the chapters treat a particular biblical passage, at least as a jumping off point for theological meditations that I hope readers will find are valid reflections of the biblical text. One of the chapters, the one on the biblical canon that is near the end of the collection, concerns one of the chief topics of my academic interests. This essay was originally written for an academic audience at a (somewhat) popular level. It will probably be a little harder to get through for some readers than the other essays, and perhaps it will seem a little out of place. For other readers, I hope it provides a gateway, or a frame of reference, for a topic of perennial fascination to people committed to the Bible and even others who are not. The final essay in the book was originally written for high schoolers, and it represents an attempt to help them think through the responsibilities of believers in an unbelieving world.

I reiterate that these chapters are attempts at approaching Christian Scripture faithfully. Readers will have to determine whether the attempts are successful. I myself am not so sure, but I've done the best I can. I hope to get better.

Endnotes

[1] Mishnah Avot 5:22. The translation is by Martin S. Jaffee in *The Oxford Annotated Mishnah*, ed. Shaye J. D. Cohen, Robert Goldenberg, and Hayim Lapin, 3 vols. (Oxford: Oxford University Press, 2022), 2.750.

[2] For two helpful and contrasting approaches to the history of biblical interpretation, see Keith D. Stanglin, *The Letter and the Spirit of Biblical Interpretation: From the Early Church to Modern Practice* (Grand Rapids: Baker, 2018); Iain Provan, *The Reformation and the Right Reading of Scripture* (Waco: Baylor University Press, 2017).

[3] On this passage, see my attempt at an explanation in *The Book of Exodus: Explorations in Christian Theology*, Cypress Bible Study Series (Florence, AL: Heritage Christian University Press, 2020), 130–37.

[4] For a brilliant and seminal account of Pauline hermeneutics, see Richard B. Hays, *Echoes of Scripture in the Letters of Paul* (New Haven: Yale University Press, 1989); and see more recently Richard B. Hays, *Echoes of Scripture in the Gospels* (Waco: Baylor University Press, 2016). For a different account of apostolic hermeneutics, see Richard N. Longenecker, *Biblical Exegesis in the Apostolic Period*, 2d ed. (Grand Rapids: Eerdmans, 1999).

[5] The leading history of the movement, with a focus on the conservative churches that call themselves churches of Christ, is Richard T. Hughes, *Reviving the Ancient Faith: The Story of Churches of Christ in America* (Grand Rapids: Eerdmans, 1996). On Stone, see D. Newell Williams, *Barton Stone: A Spiritual Biography* (St. Louis: Chalice, 2000); on Campbell, see Douglas A. Foster, *A Life of Alexander Campbell* (Grand Rapids: Eerdmans, 2020)

[6] For an exploration of the history of Bible reading within the movement, see M. Eugene Boring, *Disciples and the Bible: A History of Disciples Biblical Interpretation in North America* (St. Louis: Chalice, 1997).

[7] The sermon was printed by Campbell in his journal *Millennial Harbinger* (September 1846): 493–521.

Section 1

The Old Testament

Chapter 1

A Prostitute's Wish

Approaching 1 Kings 3[1]

I
t is a pleasure to offer this sermon from the historical books of the Bible in honor of IBC/HCU's resident historian, Wayne Kilpatrick. Wayne has taught the historical books many times, though he's known more for his work in the history of the American Restoration Movement, some elements of which are mentioned briefly in the comments below. I hope Wayne and other readers find some of these thoughts helpful for their own ministries, both in terms of ways of thinking about Scripture and ways of thinking about our current moment. Thank you, Wayne, for your life of ministry and your dedication to Christian education.

***

Solomon is a role model. When his father, David, died, and he became king, the Bible tells us, "Solomon loved the LORD" (1 Kgs 3:3). He went to the "great high place" at Gibeon to offer sacrifice (3:4). You'll recall that Gibeon is the location from which, centuries earlier, some terrified people had come to Joshua and his invading Israelite army, seeking to make a covenant, pretending to be from far away (Josh 9). To make the ruse credible, they dressed in ragged clothes and brought along stale bread. It turned out that Gibeon was actually right next to Jerusalem, about ten miles north. In the years before the Jerusalem temple was built, this town had become a place of Israelite worship. Hither came the king to make his many sacrifices out of love for his God. And God appeared to him in a dream with a dream offer: "Ask what I should give you" (3:5).

There's a scene in the movie *Three Amigos*—you remember the setup of the movie, right? A little town in Mexico (Santo Poco) is being terrorized by the infamous El Guapo, so they hire three heroes to rescue them, little realizing that these three bozos merely play heroes on the big screen. The misunderstanding goes both ways; the three actors think they've been hired to act. At any rate, the town offers them a reward. So there's a scene when all three of the Amigos—Lucky Day (Steve Martin), Dusty Bottoms (Chevy Chase), and Ned Nederlander (Martin Short)—are in a big bed about to go to sleep, when Dusty asks Lucky, "What are you going to do with your share of the reward?" Lucky says he's going to buy a shiny car, drive it around Hollywood and show off. Dusty says he's going to travel to New York and Paris and enjoy parties with lots of champagne, "be a big shot for a while." They turn to Ned and ask him, and he excitedly says, "I'm going to start a foundation to help homeless children." Dusty sheepishly replies, "That occurred to me," and Lucky explains, "I meant that I would do that first, and then buy the car."

We see this kind of question a lot, and we think about it often, too. What would you do if you won the lottery, or if you had three wishes? I don't think God came to Solomon and started singing, "You ain't never had a friend like me," but the scene in 1 Kings 3 reminds us a little bit of Aladdin with his lamp. Usually when we think of what we would do in those situations, our mind turns to the shiny car or the vacations in New York and Paris, and that's where Aladdin's mind turned, as well. He had three wishes, and—at least, according to the Disney cartoon—he was thinking of himself, how he could make life easier for himself, how he could win the heart of a princess. He did use his third wish to free the genie, so that was nice. But he did not wish for the means to start a foundation to help homeless children. He did not wish for world peace, or to end hunger. When you're in the situation, you've got one shot at giving the right answer.

Solomon gave the right answer. He asked for wisdom (3:9). He was a young king who needed help figuring out how to govern this people he was suddenly ruling. It takes wisdom to realize how much you don't know. Solomon had his one shot to give the right answer, and he did it. And for that, God gave him wisdom, but also long life and riches and honor (3:10–14). He became a great king, and people came from all around to hear his wisdom (4:29–34).

Solomon is a role model because of the great wisdom he had. Solomon is a role model for giving the right answer to God, for recognizing his own need for wisdom. Would that we turn out like Solomon!

Does that make you uncomfortable, saying that Solomon is a role model, that we should imitate him? If you know the biblical story of Solomon, you should be uncomfortable with that kind of statement. The story of Solomon is told in 1 Kings 1–11, and for the most part, it seems like he's presented as a pretty positive example, as someone pious and wise—until we get to chapter 11. That's where the wheels come off. We read that he had seven hundred wives and three hundred concubines, which seems a little excessive. And the Bible makes very clear that these wives came from places whence God had forbidden the Israelites to take wives. And these wives worshipped foreign gods (thus God's prohibition, which Solomon ignored), and Solomon built temples for these gods. The rest of the chapter shows the downward spiral, the increasing rebellion against the God who had appeared to him in a dream so many years earlier. I would suggest that if we reread the story of Solomon, we see signs, hints, earlier of how the story will turn out. For instance, even in chapter 3, where Solomon gives his wise answer and receives wisdom as a result, the chapter begins by saying that Solomon got into a political alliance with Egypt and sealed the deal through a marriage with Pharaoh's daughter. Seems like not a good idea for an Israelite king trying to follow the Torah. And he's worshipping at a high place, which the author of Kings distinguishes from the behavior of David (3:3). And a couple chapters later, Solomon starts more-or-less enslaving his own people in order to complete his building projects (5:13–18; cf. 9:20–22), a policy that would come back to bite his son, Rehoboam (12:4).

Solomon is a role model, but a complicated one. That does not make him unique; quite the opposite. I would suggest that every single character of faith in Scripture—except for one!—is at best a complicated role model, whose story makes us cringe perhaps more often than it inspires us. And that is also simply a reflection of humanity. We humans are a pretty crummy bunch. You don't need the Bible to tell you that; just look around. But the Bible agrees. On the other hand, people can be wonderful, and in 1 Kings 3, in a situation in which most of us would probably fail spectacularly (give me a car! give me a trip to Paris!), Solomon gave the best possible answer. He's certainly not all good; neither is he all bad. He's a human being.

The very next story in 1 Kings 3, Solomon gets to show off his wisdom. He's sitting as judge in his royal court in Jerusalem, and in come two prostitutes, both new mothers, but one of the babies has died. The one woman claims that the other is the mother of the dead baby, and that in the night she switched out the babies, so that now she is claiming that the living baby is hers. The other woman denies the allegation (3:17–22). How to decide who's telling the truth? Solomon calls for a sword and commands dividing the baby so that he can give each mother half (3:23–25). The trick has the desired effect: one woman relinquishes her claim on the child, saying that the king should give the child to the other woman rather than kill it (3:26). Solomon's trick is the kind of judgment that can work only once; it requires that the plaintiffs not understand that it's a trick. And we can envision situations where the trick would fail: if both women relinquish their claim on the child, or if both women plead with the king not to kill the child but continue to maintain that they are the true mother. Solomon's wisdom is displayed in his recognizing that he could get the true mother to relinquish her claim in this way. The point of the story—at least, the point of putting the story right here, after Solomon's request for wisdom—is to demonstrate that the Lord had come through, that Solomon was indeed unusually wise.

> Then the king responded: "Give the first woman the
> living boy; do not kill him. She is his mother." All Israel

heard of the judgment that the king had rendered; and they stood in awe of the king, because they perceived that the wisdom of God was in him, to execute justice (3:27–28).

What I think Solomon did not anticipate was the response of the other prostitute. Who could anticipate such a thing? "It shall be neither mine nor yours; cut it in half!" (3:26). I can picture Solomon's servants looking on in horror with mouths agape when they heard their king order the child's dissection; but when this woman spoke up, I bet they turned to her with increased horror and disgust. With her comment, the woman reveals her true motivation: it's not that she wants the child for herself, although that would probably have been the most desired outcome; rather, mostly she just wants to deprive the other woman of her child. And so she said what has to be one of the most disgusting things Solomon ever heard.

What does it take to say something like that?

Who is this woman? She is a prostitute. She lives in the same house with another prostitute (3:17), and I imagine they are not the only two, but that it is a house full of prostitutes. We have heard of houses like that. There's one, I believe, in New Orleans, called The Rising Sun, that has been the ruin of many a poor boy. She has no husband, but she has had a baby. And her baby is now dead. I have never experienced the death of a child. Alexander and Eliza Hamilton did, when their son Philip died in 1801. The loss of this child (he was 19 years old) haunted the family, sending his parents into deep grief, causing his sister unbearable mental anguish. Lin-Manuel Miranda imagines the parents, Alexander and Eliza, working through their pain with these words:

> *There are moments that the words don't reach*
> *There is suffering too terrible to name*
> *You hold your child as tight as you can*
> *And push away the unimaginable*
> *The moments when you're in so deep*
> *It feels easier to just swim down.*[2]

This woman, standing before Solomon, who had lost her baby—perhaps the greatest tragedy in a life apparently full of them—found it easier to just swim down. Let me ask you something: can you imagine yourself in her position, grieving over a dead baby, seeing another mother happy with her own baby—and hating her for it? Can you imagine yourself wishing that it had been her baby that died instead of your own? Can you imagine wishing that, since your baby has died, hers would, too? Can you imagine yourself, in misery, longing for company? I'm not trying to excuse her, but I am trying to understand her. It was exactly for situations like this that our Lord said: "Judge not, lest ye be judged. For with the standard of measurement you apply to others, so it will be measured unto you" (Matt 7:1–2).

What we cannot do is look at this woman and deny her humanity, say that she's a monster. No, that makes it too easy. The sad fact is, the person who said "cut the child in half" is not a monster, she is a human being, who shares flesh and blood with us. We must resist the temptation to make her something else, to avoid the necessary inference from Scripture. This woman is a warning to us: the human heart can sink to such depths. No, rather—the human heart often sinks to such depths. Repeatedly we see this, over and over. Take heed! She shares your flesh and blood! Inside your own heart resides the seed that she allowed to grow into a full plant bearing the fruit of hate. The problem for us is that she is not unlike us at all. It's just that she allowed herself to swim down.

This is how we need to look at every example of evil around us, as a warning to us—yes, even *that* example of evil. Even Hitler. Too often, too often, we exclaim that he was a monster. We want him to be something different from us, so that we don't have to deal with the possibility of our becoming like him. But he was not a monster, he was a human being. Hitler shared our flesh and blood. Yes, human beings can become like this. In December 1942, Dietrich Bonhoeffer was able to write to his fellow opponents of Hitler, "Nothing of what we despise in another is itself foreign to us."[3] Hitler represents to us what the human being can become when he allows hate free-reign in his heart, and meets people foolish enough to give him power to carry out his evil inclinations. Thank God we have not been given such power! "God, protect us from power. Make us weak, for we know that your power is perfected in weakness."

The movie *A Beautiful Day in the Neighborhood* is the one where Tom Hanks stars as Mr. Rogers. The movie is really about an investigative journalist who is assigned to do a profile of Mr. Rogers, and he's the kind of journalist who likes to dig up dirt on his profile subjects, exposing them as the conmen they are. He imagines that he will be able to do the same with Mr. Rogers, that he will find that Fred Rogers is just as ambitious and greedy and mean as anyone else, that he's just using this children's television show to acquire fortune and glory. There's a scene when the journalist is talking to his wife about his new profile piece, and the wife gushes about Mr. Rogers: she watched his show as a kid; she loves Mr. Rogers. And then her face grows serious as she remembers the kinds of stories her husband writes, and she appeals to him, "Please don't ruin my childhood." Spoiler: he does not ruin her childhood because Mr. Rogers turns out to be just as genuine as she had hoped. But there is truth in her comment: we expect that everybody's got some dirt. There are too many times that we've discovered that someone we thought was an example of virtue turns out to be just like us. And in some ways that's true even for the character of Mr. Rogers in this movie. Mr. Rogers has the same anger, hatred, negative emotions, as everyone else, it's just that he's more deliberate in pushing them down. He tells the journalist that when you feel the anger and hatred coming up, you can go for a swim—and then we see Mr. Rogers doing laps. He tells the journalist that another way of dealing with your negative emotions is by banging on the low end of a piano—and at the end of the movie, Mr. Rogers, at the piano, bangs all the low keys together.

Good and evil runs through the heart of all of us. Mr. Rogers shares our flesh and blood, just as much as Hitler, just as much as this broken-hearted prostitute standing in Solomon's court.

In recent years, we've been having this national conversation—actually, we've been having it for years (decades, centuries)—about race relations in America, and about monuments, and who deserves a monument. How good do they have to be? How much evil disqualifies them, or what kind of evil disqualifies them? I have opinions that I won't share here. Well, I'll share this opinion: I don't care about monuments; I'm not emotionally invested in them at all.

Tear them all down for all I care. Our Lord Jesus does not call us to make monuments to people. But I worry that this conversation we're having misleads us into thinking that there are good guys that deserve monuments and there are bad guys that don't. In some ways, that might be true. But what the Bible tells us is, there are no good guys. There is none righteous, no not one. All have turned aside; together they have become worthless.

Within churches of Christ we have our own checkered history of race relations.[4] There are moments to make you proud—moments, I said. And there are moments to make you hang your head in shame. When you read about the minstrel shows that were performed by the faculty and students at all-white schools associated with churches of Christ into the 1960s—that's the shame part. And that's not the half of it. What we cannot do is decide that these people, our forebears, are wholly different from us, that we have grown up, that we have overcome such sins. We have not. The sin of hatred, the sin of pride, the sin of anger—these we have not escaped.

This woman in King Solomon's court said something awful, thereby showing us again what humanity is all too often like. The Bible does not tell us what became of this woman; it does not say that Solomon punished her at all. I hope this was the worst thing she ever said. She did not post it on Twitter to be thrown back at her ten years later; instead it's recorded in Scripture so that for all time we know she said it. I hope she renounced those feelings; I hope she repented from that sentiment. I hope she left Solomon's court that day and lived a life of love and compassion. She was not a monster. She was a human being, which means that good and evil flowed through her heart, just as it flowed through the heart of the king who rendered that wise judgment that day, just as it flows through all of our hearts. She shared with us flesh and blood.

Our hope is not in overcoming our flesh and blood; our hope is not in being better people than anyone else. Our hope is that Jesus also shared our flesh and blood, so that he might become a merciful and faithful high priest, "to make a sacrifice of atonement for the sins of the people" (Heb 2:14–17). We have plenty of stories in Scripture and outside of Scripture that warn us of what people made of flesh and blood can become. Thank God, the story of Jesus also shows us what people made of flesh and blood can become.

***

There can be no genuine knowledge of sin that does not lead me down to this depth. If my sin appears to me to be in any way smaller or less reprehensible in comparison with the sins of others, then I am not yet recognizing my sin at all. My sin is of necessity the worst, the most serious, the most objectionable. Christian love will find any number of excuses for the sins of others; only for my sin is there no excuse whatsoever.[5]

Endnotes

[1] This chapter first appeared in *Things Most Surely Believed: Festschrift for C. Wayne Kilpatrick*, Heritage Legacy Series, (Florence, AL: Heritage Christian University Press, 2021).

[2] From the song "It's Quiet Uptown," from the musical *Hamilton* (2015). See also the reflections on "sinking down" in ch. 1 of James Cone's *The Cross and the Lynching Tree*

(Maryknoll, NY: Orbis, 2011): "To sink down was to give up on life and embrace hopelessness," in conversation with blues music. Cone also cites Kierkegaard's definition of the Sickness unto Death as despair. Augustine at one time regarded despair as the sin against the Holy Spirit; see discussion in Peter Brown, *Augustine of Hippo: A Biography* (London: Faber & Faber, 1967), 152.

³ Bonhoeffer's Christmas letter titled "After Ten Years," in the section of the letter called "Contempt for Humanity?" I have used the translation in *Letters and Papers from Prison*, Dietrich Bonhoeffer Works 8 (Minneapolis: Fortress, 2010), 45.

⁴ See, for instance, Edward J. Robinson, *Hard-Fighting Soldiers: A History of African American Churches of Christ* (Knoxville: University of Tennessee Press, 2019); Barclay Key, *Race and Restoration: Churches of Christ and the Black Freedom Struggle* (Baton Rouge: Louisiana State University Press, 2020).

⁵ Dietrich Bonhoeffer, *Life Together* (1939), trans. Daniel W. Bloesch, ed. Geffrey B. Kelly, Dietrich Bonhoeffer Works 5 (Minneapolis: Fortress, 1996), 97–98, meditating on Paul's claim to be the chief of sinners (1 Tim 1:15).

Chapter 2

A Still Small Voice
Approaching 1 Kings 19[1]

B ill Bagents has had an enormous influence on Heritage Christian University and on me personally. He gave me my first full-time job and was my boss for more than a decade, fostering a wonderful environment in which I and others could grow spiritually and professionally. I am grateful for his service to our little school and for the example of teaching and ministry that he has set for me and others. It is my pleasure to offer him this sermon in gratitude.

***

In 1 Kings 19, Elijah is scared. His life has been threatened by Jezebel, Israel's queen (19:2), and so he flees, runs south, first to Judah (19:3), and eventually to Horeb (19:8), the alternative name for Mount Sinai.[2] A messenger sent by Jezebel announced her intention to have the prophet killed. Elijah runs, sits under a tree, and bemoans his situation: "It is enough; now, O LORD, take away my life, for I am no better than my fathers" (19:4).

Bible teachers and preachers often diagnose Elijah with depression in this story, so it is important for the reader to understand that I do not share this viewpoint. I will say some things about Elijah that I would not say to or about a person suffering from depression. Depression is a serious matter, and someone who suffers from depression needs medical and psychological help. It may be that Elijah was experiencing depression in 1 Kings 19, but I do not think this is clear at all, and I myself read the story as not about depression but rather about whining—two completely different emotional conditions warranting two completely different responses. (For more, see the supplement at the end of this chapter.) Probably part of the reason I don't interpret Elijah as depressed in this chapter is that I have no experience with depression (certainly not of the diagnosable variety), whereas I do have a lot of experience with whining. I have six children, and they have helped me become an expert on whining. I have even done some of it myself.

No Better than My Fathers

What does Elijah mean—"I am no better than my fathers"? We have seen movies where lines like this have made an appearance: "I'll never be like my father." Maybe we ourselves have said such things in our younger days. Maybe in our late teenage years or our early twenties, we have vowed not to imitate our parents in certain ways. "My father treated his kids in such-and-such a way; I'll never do that to my kids!" Or: "My father treated his wife in a particular way, or was involved in some bad habit, and I'll never do that!" Oftentimes people who say such things fail to live up to their ideals. They end up doing the very things they vowed to avoid, just like their old man. It turns out, they're no better than their fathers.

The movie *The Godfather*, the first one, is all about exploring this precise concept. At the beginning of the movie, Michael Corleone (Al Pacino) is declaring to his love interest, Kay (Diane Keaton), that though his family is a bunch of criminals, he's not going to be like them. He's got ideals. He's going to be better than his fathers. Of course, he's wrong. He's no better than his fathers. The final scene of the movie shows Michael being addressed as "Godfather" and closing the door on his wife, Kay.

But Elijah can't mean that, can he? Surely Elijah is much better than his fathers. After all, Elijah's fathers were pagans, idol-worshippers, and Elijah has fought his whole life to convince the Israelites to worship only the Lord rather than Baal or some other god. Elijah is better than his fathers, isn't he? I guess it depends on who his fathers are. Maybe Elijah doesn't mean by "fathers" his actual, biological ancestors, or even Israelites of previous generations, but—more narrowly—former prophets. Maybe what Elijah means is that he's no better at being a prophet than the previous prophets were, no better at demonstrating the absurdity of worshiping Baal, no better at calling the Israelites to faithfulness. Maybe Elijah had thought that where the earlier prophets failed he would succeed. Maybe he imagined his prophetic career as continually chipping away at Israelite idolatry until he made such an impressive demonstration of the correctness of worshiping the Lord over worshiping Baal that no one would be able to deny it.

Elijah had certainly made an impressive demonstration. In the previous chapter (1 Kgs 18), we read about the contest of Mount Carmel, when Elijah challenged the 450 prophets

of Baal (and the 400 prophets of Asherah; 18:19) to a compe-
tition among their respective deities. The prophets of Baal
built an altar, and prayed, and cut themselves, and were
mocked by Elijah. "Perhaps Baal is using the bathroom.
Perhaps he's on vacation" (18:27). Baal did not answer the
cry of his prophets. But Elijah's simple prayer (18:36–37)
was answered by a fire from heaven that consumed the
animal sacrifice and the altar and the water in the trench
around the altar (18:38). The choice between Baal and the
Lord was clearly no real choice at all, and the people finally
got it! "The LORD indeed is God; the LORD indeed is
God" (18:39). And at that moment Elijah had accumulated
such authority that he could order the deaths of those
prophets of Baal, in accordance with Mosaic legislation
(Deut 13:5). The people of Israel, who ten minutes earlier
had been worshipers of Baal under the influence of these
same prophets, were the ones who put the false prophets to
death (18:40).

Elijah may well have felt as if this moment on Mount
Carmel was the culmination of his career—nay, more, the
culmination of all previous Israelite prophecy. Other
prophets had labored in vain to achieve something like this,
such a compelling demonstration of the Lord's power and of
the emptiness of Baal, which had actually worked to turn the
Israelites around so that they worshiped the Lord. The
outcome that all the prophets had been hoping to attain had
finally been accomplished by Elijah. He could now live
happily ever after, relishing his great victory that changed
Israelite history forever.

And then he received this message from the Israelite
queen: "May the gods do to me and more also if by this time
tomorrow I do not make your life like the lives of them"

(19:2). Jezebel was referring to those dead prophets of Baal, and threatening Elijah with a similar fate. She was going to have him killed.

Elijah realized that his great victory was going to last all of about a day. He had not succeeded, after all, in convincing everyone to put away their Baal idols. He had done everything he knew how to do—he could not possibly outdo the contest on Mount Carmel—and it wasn't good enough. He realized that he was no better than his fathers. He realized that there would be no great victory followed by a "happily ever after." His life would be a constant battle.

So we find our lives reflected in the experience of Elijah, for we too desire the great victory and the "happily ever after" only to find that great victory always just out of reach. Life is a lot like doing the dishes (or the laundry)—you never get to a point where you have done them all. There are always more dishes to do. When you clean the floors of your house, it won't be long until you have to clean them again. So also in our spiritual lives: the struggle against sin is constant; the need to read Scripture, to pray, to grow closer to God, is never fully satisfied. Christ continually calls us closer to Him. No final victories in this life relieve us of the responsibility to struggle against the false gods around us.

How does God respond to Elijah's lament that he is no better than his fathers? Had we been there, I think we would have been tempted to encourage him with something like, "Oh, yes, you are! You're a really good prophet! Why, there are a lot of prophets that wish they had as much success as you!" God leaves the complaint unaddressed; he ignores it, which in itself is a kind of response, something like, "so what?" God did not call Elijah as His prophet because He thought Elijah would be better than previous prophets. He knew what He was getting with Elijah, and even if Elijah is disappointed in himself for not getting the results he hoped for, there's nothing to suggest that God is disappointed in Elijah. "You're not better than your fathers? Yeah, I know. You're just now realizing that?"

Power and Fear

The reason Elijah has now acknowledged that he is no better than his fathers is because he has received a message from Jezebel. By the way, how would you like to be this messenger? You've got to deliver a threatening message to a prophet who has just called down fire from heaven. This is the prophet who has just ordered the execution of hundreds of Baal prophets. I think if I were the messenger, I'd be a little intimidated. It reminds me of the first *Ip Man* film (2008). Our title character is a Chinese martial arts expert, the legendary teacher of Bruce Lee. During World War II, when China was invaded by Japanese forces, Ip Man had occasion to get into a fight with some Japanese experts in martial arts. In one scene, Ip Man defeated about twenty Japanese fellows all at once, and there was one Japanese guy left who had not joined the fight. I think after seeing what Ip Man had done to all those other guys, I might just say, "No need to fight. You win." But this Japanese fellow doesn't do that; he goes into battle against Ip Man and receives his beating. I bet the messenger delivering the death threat to Elijah was just hoping to survive the encounter.

Come to think of it, why is Jezebel sending Elijah this messenger? Why does she send a guy with a message rather than a guy with a sword? If you wanted to kill somebody— not that you'd ever do such a thing, but I'm sure as you've watched movies that involve a murder, the thought has crossed your mind about what mistakes the murderer should avoid—if you wanted to kill somebody, would you send them a message about it, first? Seems like the message might, you know, tip them off. In May 2011, when those Navy SEALs raided the compound of Osama bin Laden and dispatched the terrorist, do you think they sent him a message, first? Do you think they let him know that they were coming for him? Seems unlikely.

So why didn't Jezebel just send in SEAL Team Six rather than issue a press release? I'll tell you why—she was bluffing. Jezebel understood that she had no power over Elijah, that Elijah had access to power that she knew nothing about. Jezebel has no prophet who can call down fire from heaven. The complete impotence of her prophets and of her god was painfully revealed on Mount Carmel. Jezebel is scared of Elijah; she knows he's the real deal. All she can do is send a guy to declare: "Oh yeah, well ... I'm gonna kill you!" Of course, she wasn't really going to try to assassinate Elijah. Jezebel recognizes that Elijah is out of her league.

But Elijah does not recognize what Jezebel sees so clearly. He receives a death threat, and he runs away scared. To say it again, he had just shown all Israel that he was a prophet of the true God, who controls heaven and earth, who has infinitely more power than other gods. Elijah has no business being intimidated by a message from this queen. He has access to power that she cannot imagine. And he runs away in fear.

Yet again, life imitates Elijah. We too, brothers and sisters, have access to power that the world cannot imagine, and we often live in fear. Of course, none of us are calling down fire from heaven—that's usually not the kind of power

God cares to grant us. But think through this declaration: "His divine power has given us everything we need for life and godliness through the knowledge of him who called us by his own glory and goodness" (2 Pet 1:3). Our context is different from that of Elijah. We are not conquering in any sort of physical way; that is not what the New Testament calls us to, certainly not what the example of Jesus displays. We are not going to pick up swords and slay the false prophets. So how can God's power be manifested in us? Just like Jesus, we endure, without complaint (Mark 15:1–5; Phil 4:13!). Just like Paul and Silas, when we face opposition, we sing praises (Acts 16:19–25). Through our knowledge of him who called us, we understand the nature of this life, and what is coming next. By the power of God, we can say, to live is Christ, and to die is gain (Phil 1:21).

We have no business submitting to fear (1 John 4:18), which is usually (always?) a sign that our hopes and dreams do not align with those of God—which also seems to have been Elijah's problem.

God's Gentle Rebuke

When Elijah gets to Horeb, God asks him what he's doing, to which Elijah responds:

> I have been very zealous for the LORD, the God of hosts; for the Israelites have forsaken your covenant, thrown down your altars, and killed your prophets with the sword. I alone am left, and they are seeking my life, to take it away (1 Kgs 19:10).

He repeats this same comments at 19:14, and the apostle

Paul finds occasion to quote part of this speech at Romans 11:3. The apostle points out that, strictly speaking, Elijah's statement is incorrect; he's not the only one left.

> But what is the divine reply to him? "I have kept for myself seven thousand who have not bowed the knee to Baal" (Rom 11:4, quoting 1 Kgs 19:18).

There are more worshipers of the Lord than merely Elijah, at least 7000 more. Now, maybe Elijah meant that he was the only prophet of the Lord left (cf. 1 Kgs 18:22), but that's actually not correct either. We've already been told that a fellow named Obadiah, a courtier to Ahab, had protected a hundred prophets (18:4) from the murderous rage of Jezebel.

So Elijah is not the only one, but at least he feels like he's the only one—which prompts God to reveal Himself to his prophet, this time not in fire from heaven as at Mount Carmel.

> He said, "Go out and stand on the mountain of the LORD, for the LORD is about to pass by." [We are reminded of Exod 33:21–34:8, which took place at the same mountain.] Now there was a great wind, so strong that it was splitting mountains and breaking rocks in pieces before the LORD, but the LORD was not in the wind; and after the wind an earthquake, but the LORD was not in the earthquake; and after the earthquake a fire, but the LORD was not in the fire; and after the fire a sound of sheer silence (1 Kgs 19:11–12).

More familiar than the NRSV's "sound of sheer silence"

is the KJV's "still small voice." God is not in the great wind, or the earthquake, or the fire, but in the whisper. If the Lord is not in the three previous phenomena, why mention them at all? It seems to be a reference to an earlier time when Horeb or Mount Sinai—was at the center of the biblical narrative. When God rescued Israel from Egyptian slavery and brought them to Mount Sinai, He manifested Himself in a thunderstorm and fire and an earthquake.

> On the morning of the third day there was thunder and lightning, as well as a thick cloud on the mountain, and a blast of a trumpet so loud that all the people who were in the camp trembled. Moses brought the people out of the camp to meet God. They took their stand at the foot of the mountain. Now Mount Sinai was wrapped in smoke, because the LORD had descended upon it in fire; the smoke went up like the smoke of a kiln, while the whole mountain shook violently. As the blast of the trumpet grew louder and louder, Moses would speak and God would answer him in thunder (Exod 19:16–19).

The appearance of God had the desired effect: the people were scared to death and begged Moses to intercede for them (Exod 20:18–19). God showed himself as all-powerful and worthy of reverence. This sort of manifestation of God is what the psalm-writer has in mind.

> *Our God comes and does not keep silence,*
> *before him is a devouring fire,*
> *and a mighty tempest all around him (Ps*
> *50:3).*

When Elijah experiences the earthquake and the wind and the fire at Horeb, the experience apparently references the earlier manifestation of God on Sinai. But the text of 1 Kings explicitly says that God was not in these phenomena, but rather in the "still small voice." Why the difference between Exodus 19 and 1 Kings 19 in the manner of God's self-revelation? Presumably the answer is that the Lord wanted to distinguish himself firmly from Baal, the god that had just been decisively defeated on Mount Carmel. The Lord did not want anyone to confuse him with Baal, who was a weather god, controlling the thunder storm.[3] Though the Lord at one time revealed himself through thunder and lightning, at this time on Horeb he decided to leave that symbolism behind and reveal himself in as different a way as he could.

What did the whisper say? Have you ever asked yourself that question? The text does not reveal it, so any answer we give would be a guess. Still, I think it might be worth guessing. When God came to whisper in the ear of His prophet— His prophet who was lamenting his failure to change every heart in Israel in one fell swoop, His prophet who was complaining about being the only one left who remained true to God—what did He say? My suggestion: God gently whispered, "Get over yourself."

If we interpret 1 Kings 19 as a story about a prophet who was whining (rather than a story about a prophet who was clinically depressed), I think the prophet probably needed to hear that message. "Get over yourself. You think you're the only one left? You think everything depends on you, that if I didn't have you on my side that all my plans would fall apart? You think you're the only one who represents what is good? Let me tell you something: I've got seven thousand more. You are not the one essential person. You need to get over yourself."

We, too, need to hear this message sometimes. Do you know people who think that the work of the church rests almost solely on their shoulders, that if they didn't show up the church would fall apart? Or maybe they think their ideas are not only the best ideas but essential, so that if people—a congregation, or a church program, or whatever—follow the advice of someone else, if their ideas are not implemented, we might as well shut the doors. They need to get over themselves. If they don't get their way, God's kingdom will be ... just fine.

The apostle Paul likes to depict God's people as a collection of body parts that together make up the body of Christ. Some people are hands and some people are eyes and some people are other parts, and when everyone performs their own role well, the body functions as God designed it to.[4] One time I heard a preacher tell some people at a church retreat, in reflecting on this imagery from Paul, to try to name at least ten body parts that had three-letter names (e.g., leg, arm, eye; you can google the rest). He then asked the people to get in groups and think about what these body parts have in common. Do you have an answer to that? My answer at the time, and I still think it's a good one, was: they're all expendable. It would stink to go through life without an eye, or a leg, or an arm, but I've seen people do it. Certain body parts are indispensable, and no body part can be removed without pain. But the fact is you can live without certain body parts. They are expendable. When we think about the body of Christ, am I an indispensable body part, or an expendable body part? An honest and self-aware answer can only put me in the latter category. God can get along without me. The church can get along without me—even if my loss would cause a certain amount of suffering to the body. If I think I'm indispensable, I probably need God to whisper in my ear, "Get over yourself."

Sometimes we need to be reminded of the words of Eliza Doolittle.

> *They can still rule with land without you.*
> *Windsor Castle will stand without you.*
> *And without much ado we can all muddle*
>   *through without you.*

Let's admit that it's often church leaders and especially preachers that need to hear God's whisper. Sometimes a minister's incorrect perception that he's indispensable contributes to a toxic environment,[5] or even something beyond toxic. Unfortunately, evidence is not hard to come by. Which famous preacher who has brought shame upon himself and his ministry should I name? Let's go with Ravi Zacharias, whose apologetics books and lectures helped many Christians understand their faith better within the modern world, and who abused many women over the course of his long career. He died early in 2020, a few months before the allegations against him became more prominent. It turns out the allegations had been made many times over the years, only to be swept under the rug and hidden by nondisclosure agreements. In an essay on the allegations, David French correctly criticized the motivation behind these cover-ups.

> The zeal to protect the leader and punish or discredit the accuser can also rest in a particular brand of arrogance.

"My ministry is necessary." "Souls are at stake." "Look at all the good we're doing." In reality, God will accomplish His purposes, with or without any of us, regardless of our gifts or talents.[6]

As always, the words of Dietrich Bonhoeffer warrant contemplation.

> Only those who live by the forgiveness of their sin in Jesus Christ will think little of themselves in the right way. They will know that their own wisdom completely came to an end when Christ forgave them. They remember the cleverness of the first human beings, who wanted to know what is good and evil and died in this cleverness. The first person, however, who was born on this earth was Cain, the murderer of his brother. His crime is the fruit of humanity's wisdom. Because they can no longer consider themselves wise, Christians will also have a modest opinion of their own plans and intentions. They will know that it is good for their own will to be broken in their encounter with their neighbor. They will be ready to consider their neighbor's will more important and urgent than their own. What does it matter if our own plans are thwarted? Is it better to serve our neighbor than to get our own way?[7]

God wanted Elijah to have a proper perception of his role in the world. Everything did not depend on him. He was not the only one left. Whatever God whispered in the prophet's ear (1 Kgs 19:12), Elijah renewed his complaints (19:14), which prompted God's final speech in this chapter (19:15–18). The Lord instructed his prophet to get to work:

anoint the next king of Aram (fulfilled at 2 Kgs 8:7–15), anoint the next king of Israel (fulfilled at 2 Kgs 9:1–10), and anoint his own successor (fulfilled later in the chapter, 19:19–21). These instructions to Elijah assure him and us both (1) that God has a plan for the short term and the long term, even if we don't know what it is; and (2) that rather than wallowing in what we think of as our failures (an opinion God might not share, as presumably in the case of Elijah) we should focus on the next task in front of us and allow God to work everything out according to his pleasure—just as he promises he will do (Rom 8:28).

It is probably the case that we're no better than our fathers. Struggling with personal insecurities is part of the human condition. But let's not allow such an insignificant evaluation of ourselves to distract us from the mission in front of us. Let's live without fear and with confidence—not in ourselves but in the God whose divine power has granted us everything we need for life and godliness.

Endnotes

[1] This essay first appeared in *Fighting the Good Fight: A Festschrift for Bill Bagents*, Heritage Legacy Series, (Florence, AL: Heritage Christian University Press, 2022). I appreciate Brad McKinnon's careful reading of this essay and his valuable suggestions for its improvement.

[2] On the name "Horeb," see Ed Gallagher, *The Book of Exodus: Explorations in Christian Theology*, Cypress Bible Study Series (Florence, AL: Heritage Christian University Press, 2020), 25. For the location of the mountain, see p. 24 note 4.

[3] For a description of Baal, see Michael Hundley,

Yahweh among the Gods: The Divine in Genesis, Exodus, and the Ancient Near East (Cambridge: Cambridge University Press, 2022), 158–59.

[4] Paul's most developed account of this imagery is in 1 Corinthians 12; cf. Romans 12:4–5; 1 Corinthians 6:15; 10:17; Ephesians 1:23; 2:16; 4:4, 11–16; 5:23, 30; Colossians 1:18; 2:19; 3:15;

[5] Have you listened to the podcast called *The Rise and Fall of Mars Hill*, produced by Christianity Today?

[6] David French, "You Are Only One Step Away from Complete and Total Insanity," *TheDispatch.com*, February 14, 2021.

[7] Dietrich Bonhoeffer, *Life Together* (1939), trans. Daniel W. Bloesch, ed. Geffrey B. Kelly, Dietrich Bonhoeffer Works 5 (Minneapolis: Fortress, 1996), 96.

Supplement to Chapter 2
Was Elijah Depressed?

According to the *Diagnostic and Statistical Manual of Mental Disorders*, a diagnosis of depression can result from the presence of at least five of the following nine symptoms for a 2-week period.[1]

1. Depressed mood most of the day, nearly every day, as indicated by either subjective report (e.g., feels sad, empty, hopeless) or observation made by others (e.g., appears tearful).

2. Markedly diminished interest or pleasure in all, or almost all, activities most of the day, nearly every day (as indicated by either subjective account or observation).

3. Significant weight loss when not dieting or weight gain (e.g., a change of more than 5% of body weight in a month), or decrease or increase in appetite nearly every day.

4. Insomnia or hypersomnia nearly every day.

5. Psychomotor agitation or retardation nearly every day (observable by others, not merely subjective feelings of restlessness or being slowed down).

6. Fatigue or loss of energy nearly every day.

7. Feelings of worthlessness or excessive or inappropriate guilt (which may be delusional) nearly every day (not merely self-reproach or guilt about being sick).

8. Diminished ability to think or concentrate, or indecisiveness, nearly every day (either by subjective account or as observed by others).
9. Recurrent thoughts of death (not just fear of dying), recurrent suicidal ideation without a specific plan, or a suicide attempt or a specific plan for committing suicide.

Did Elijah manifest these symptoms in 1 Kings 19? There are certainly some similarities. But the whole chapter is not really relevant to a diagnosis of this type, as far as I can tell. The only passage at play is 19:4–7, because after that point, Elijah is doing merely what God directs (e.g., go here, answer this question). Elijah does express a desire for death at 19:4, but not after that point. And if he refrains from eating for more than a month, it's owing to the instruction of God (19:8).

At 19:4–7, was Elijah experiencing depression? One point to consider is that the symptoms we might find in this passage apparently last only a single day (19:4), not the two weeks required for a diagnosis. But did he experience the symptoms of depression even for a single day?

1. Depressed mood? Yes
2. Diminished interest in activities? Sure, I guess
3. Weight loss? Uhh, over the course of a day? Not really, but maybe he didn't eat much that day. The angel does tell him to eat.
4. Insomnia? Again, it's just a day, but sure, maybe he hadn't slept and that's why he sleeps so much in the wilderness.

5. Psychomotor agitation or retardation? Is Elijah fidgety (or the opposite of that)? I don't think we have enough information to say.
6. Fatigue? Well, he's sleeping, so maybe. Then again, he has been traveling (19:3–4). One might expect a depressed person lacking energy to not flee from Jezebel at all.
7. Feelings of worthlessness? Yes.
8. Indecisiveness? Maybe.
9. Recurrent thoughts of death? Thoughts of death, yes. Recurrent? There's no indication of that.

Did we get at least five symptoms? We got two "yeses" and several "maybes." That suggests to me that it is reasonable to imagine that Elijah is experiencing the symptoms of depression here (but probably not for the two weeks required for a diagnosis), and—given the uncertainty regarding most of the diagnostic indicators—it is reasonable to interpret Elijah as not experiencing the symptoms of depression. It could be that if we knew more about Elijah, especially his life prior to his threat from Jezebel, we would be able to diagnose him with something—if not depression, perhaps Acute Stress Disorder or some Adjustment Disorders. The biblical account does not give us the kinds of details that we would need to be confident in a diagnosis.

If you or someone you know experiences most of these symptoms for more than a week, seek help. Clinical depression is not something to take lightly, not something that most people can just "get over" by looking on the bright side. It is a sickness that needs to be treated, usually through therapy, sometimes through medication. Church leaders, encourage people exhibiting these symptoms to seek professional help and aid them in getting that help. That is how you are going to love your neighbor.

Endnotes

[1] *Diagnostic and Statistical Manual of Mental Disorders*, 5th ed. (Washington, DC: American Psychiatric Publishing, 2013), 160–61. I appreciate the help of Rosemary Snodgrass and Jeffrey Brothers with this discussion, though I doubt I have convinced either of them of my psychological analysis.

Chapter 3

A Time for Defiance
Approaching Esther 3[1]

I f only Mordecai had bowed to Haman, he would have saved himself a lot of trouble and his people would have been spared near-genocide. Mordecai was defiant.

Defiance is always costly. The unbelieving world around us does not like defiance; it likes conformity. In the twenty-first century, we constantly hear the message that we need to resist conformity, that we need to be ourselves, express our individual identity. But, of course, this resistance to conformity, this self-expression, must conform to the acceptable limits, or else social media will reveal to you what society thinks of your self-expression. It's reminiscent of high school kids whose teenage rebellion all looks exactly the same: they're all wearing the same clothes and listening to the same music and fixing their hair in the same way. As Carl Trueman says, "The teenager who wants to express her freedom does so by wearing the uniform of the group to which she wishes to belong."[2] They know they must defy convention in very conventional ways or they will pay a steep price.

Defiance is the natural posture for the believer in reference to the world. We live in a world in rebellion against God, and so it has always been. Jesus was born into a world in rebellion against God, and he lived his life in defiance of that world. Jesus was born into a religion of which some of the most powerful practitioners were—perhaps unconsciously, certainly without public acknowledgment of the fact—in rebellion against God. Jesus was defiant of them. He paid a steep price. He also insisted that his followers imitate his example, assured that they would pay a similar price.

Mordecai's Defiance

Esther 3 begins by introducing readers to a new character, Haman the Agagite. There is no known ethnicity of Agagites, but the term probably echoes the name of the Amalekite king, Agag, mentioned in 1 Samuel 15:8. In that chapter, Saul, king of Israel, was commanded to destroy the Amalekites, but he spared some of the animals and the king (15:20–21), so Samuel the prophet killed Agag (15:33). The description of Haman as an Agagite probably identifies him as a descendant of a people once massacred by Israel, so that Haman is the bearer of an ancient grudge.

Ahasuerus (Xerxes), king of Persia, promoted Haman to a position over all the other officials. This action itself may remind readers of Daniel 6, where Darius the Mede had already appointed Daniel to a top position and was planning to advance him even higher when he made a foolish law that resulted in his favorite official being sentenced to a night in a den of lions. It was Daniel's defiance that earned him that night with the lions, because he refused to conform his religious practices to the dictates of a fickle world. In Esther 3, we quickly learn that Haman is exactly opposite Daniel, not at all defiant of the fickle world but greedy for its rewards.

The king has commanded everyone to do obeisance before Haman, to bow in his presence. Of course, everyone is only too eager to obey the king's command and bow before Haman—everyone except Mordecai. (Again, we are reminded of a story in Daniel, this time in chapter 3 and involving Shadrach, Meshach, and Abednego.) Mordecai refuses, but the text does not say why. Bowing before a political superior seems like a fairly mild thing to do. Abraham bows before the sons of Heth (Gen 23:7, 12), and Moses bowed to his father-in-law (Exod 18:7). I wouldn't be surprised to learn that Christians in countries with a royal family conventionally bow if they are ever in the presence of a member of the royal family. We typically use respectful forms of address for people in high positions. It does not strike me as obviously sinful to bow before a person in some circumstances.

Mordecai refused to bow. I can think of two possible reasons, and maybe you can think of others. Perhaps Mordecai would not bow specifically to Haman, or perhaps he would not bow to any human being. If the issue was Haman specifically, I suppose we must imagine that Mordecai knew the moral character of Haman from previous interactions or reports, and he did not consider Haman worthy of a show of respect. If the issue was not Haman specifically, perhaps Mordecai felt that bowing before any human was inappropriate or even sinful because only God deserves such honor (cf. Acts 10:25–26).[3]

Whatever the precise reason, imagine the scene: out comes Haman, with pomp and circumstance, and everyone bows except for one man. Mordecai knew he would face repercussions. Even if he was not aware of the character of Haman the individual, he surely knew how most high-level political appointees bristled at any perceived sleight—and in this case the sleight was not merely perceived but obvious to all. He must have known while he was standing amid a kneeling crowd that he would soon experience pain.

Similar acts of defiance have become indelibly imprinted on our minds. We've seen the news footage and the reenactments of the crossing of the Edmund Pettus bridge on March 7, 1965, an act of defiance that triggered immediate retribution. As courageous as this march was, the protestors could find comfort in community as hundreds participated. Mordecai's action might remind us more of "Tank Man," the lone man (still unidentified) who blocked the paths of the tanks during the Tiananmen Square protests (June 5, 1989).

We can expect that such actions of defiance will often be lonely. Of course, the broader culture will be against you—otherwise it would be more an act of conformity than defiance. But even religious people that you might think should support you will often either remain silent or actively oppose you. Shadrach, Meshach, and Abednego had each other, but apparently no one else. There were no doubt many Jews in Daniel 3 that wished they did not have to bow down to Nebuchadnezzar's statue but were unwilling to pay the terrible price of disobedience. Jesus faced fierce opposition, especially among the religious elite.

The story is told (especially in 2 Maccabees) that in the days of the Greek king Antiochus IV Epiphanes, in the first half of the second century BC, the king basically outlawed the practice of Judaism—and he was encouraged to pursue this course by some Jews, some of the religious elite! Other Jews were defiant, but in resisting the king's orders they stood opposed not only to the Greeks but to many of their own countrymen.

A few centuries later, 86-year-old Polycarp, a Christian, was sentenced to death for his refusal to give proper honor to Caesar. The story is found in a document called *The Martyrdom of Polycarp*.[4] When some people tried to convince Polycarp that there was no harm in offering incense while saying, "Caesar is Lord," Polycarp simply responded, "I am not about to do what you are suggesting to me" (8.2).[5] Later, the proconsul commanded him, "Swear by the genius of Caesar; repent; say, 'Away with the atheists!'" (9.2). The proconsul referred to the Christians as atheists because they refused to acknowledge the traditional Roman gods.[6] Polycarp turned the charge around.

> So Polycarp solemnly looked at the crowd of lawless heathen who were in the stadium, motioned toward them with his hand, and then (groaning as he looked up to heaven) said, "Away with the atheists!"

The proconsul gave Polycarp another chance: "Swear the oath, and I will release you; revile Christ!" (9:3). Polycarp finally gave a full reply:

> If you vainly suppose that I will swear by the genius of Caesar, and pretend not to know who I am, listen carefully: I am a Christian. Now if you want to learn the doctrine of Christianity, name a day and give me a hearing (10.1).

When the proconsul finally relented and turned Polycarp over to death by fire in the stadium, he introduced the old man to the crowd, announcing that he had confessed to being a Christian. The crowd then shouted that Polycarp was "the destroyer of the gods" (10.2)—an honorable title to carry into the hereafter to meet the Lord.

Polycarp paid a hefty price in order to earn his title "destroyer of the gods." He claimed to have been the servant of Jesus for eighty-six years (9.3), and no doubt he had lived a life in defiance against the culture around him, and that's what led to his capture in the first place. But then, when given the opportunity to capitulate to the powers-that-be or to suffer the slings and arrows of outrageous fortune, he chose service to God and defiance against the enemies of God. In order to honor his God, he welcomed the fire prepared for his death and the sword that eventually killed him (chs. 14–16). Polycarp stood alone in that moment, and he suffered immense pain. Such was the cost of his defiance.

Mordecai also stood alone, and he suffered terribly for his defiance. Yes, Mordecai's story is a "happily ever after" tale, showing a God who redeems his people through the most trying circumstances. But the redemption came only after much emotional and psychological pain, arising from Haman's ridiculously vindictive plan to eliminate the entire Jewish population from Persia. (Unfortunately, such a plan is not unique to Haman.) Mordecai's defiance of wicked Haman brought him near to death, but as Jesus says in the book of Revelation (another book all about defiance), "be thou faithful unto death, and I will give thee a crown of life" (Rev 2:10).

When Is the Time for Defiance?

When Alexander Campbell as a young adult spent some months in Scotland before finally immigrating to America, he found himself doubting the claims of the Seceder Presbyterian Church, into which he had been born as the son of an ordained minister. The church provided the Lord's Supper only twice in a year, and when the semi-annual event approached, Campbell wondered whether to participate. To ensure that only members in good standing partook of the emblems, the Church required each congregant to have a metallic token, an admission ticket of sorts.[7] Campbell earned his token by passing an oral theology examination,

> but when the hour of the celebration of the Lord's Supper arrived, his scruples overcame him, and instead of taking his place among the communicants, he cast his token into the plate that was passed around, and declined to partake with the rest. The ring of that token, as it fell from his hands, like the ring of Martin Luther's hammer on the door of the Wittenberg cathedral, announced his renunciation of the old church ties, and marks the moment at which he forever ceased to recognise the claims or authority of a human creed to bind upon men the conditions of their acceptance with God.[8]

According to Earl West, this was the moment when Campbell "crossed the rubicon."[9]

This way of telling the story of Campbell's forgoing the Lord's Supper in Scotland presents it as an act of defiance that—like Luther's 95 Theses—precipitated a great religious reformation. Like Mordecai and Polycarp, so also Luther and

Campbell resolutely stood against the political and ecclesiastical powers of their days and determined to lead an opposition movement.

Then again, a little reading about what Luther was trying to accomplish on October 31, 1517, generates some doubt about whether he thought he was decisively standing against the ecclesiastical hierarchy by wielding the hammer that day. His famous statement "Here I stand. I can do no other. God help me" (if he actually said it) is attributed to the meeting he had with Charles V, Holy Roman Emperor, in 1521, by which time much had changed since 1517. Apparently, what Luther thought he was doing by nailing his 95 Theses to the door of the Wittenberg chapel was starting a conversation about the propriety of indulgences; he had no intention of starting a reformation movement, only suggesting some reforms. I do not mean that taking up the hammer was not an act of courage—it was—but it was not the decisive action from immovable conviction that in hindsight it appeared to be. Or, perhaps we should say that hindsight gives us the better view, and no matter what Luther thought he was doing that day, when he acted with whatever conviction he had in order to bring about whatever small goals he contemplated, even that small act of defiance changed the course of history.

Likewise, Campbell. Grafton and West tell a dramatic story of his tossing his token in the plate in order to signal to all around him that he was done with Protestant parties. According to West, Campbell thus crossed the rubicon. It is doubtful whether Campbell realized he had made such a crossing. The version of this story recorded in Richardson's *Memoirs of Alexander Campbell* also sets a dramatic scene but finishes the tale by acknowledging,

This change, however, was as yet confined to his own heart. He was young, and thought it unbecoming to make known publicly his objections, and as he had fully complied with all the rules of the Church, he thought it proper to receive at his departure the usual certificate of good standing.[10]

Surely the token incident was significant to Campbell, and he reflected on it in later years, but at the time its full significance was not manifest, probably not even to Campbell.

The point I'm trying to make is that not every act of defiance must be as dramatic and decisive as Mordecai's or Polycarp's. Campbell and Luther provide examples of defiance that—once historical research dissipates the glow of hagiography—are actually very prosaic, even quotidian. These are helpful examples to us. Believers need to adopt a quotidian posture of defiance.

I have said that the believer's natural posture toward the world is defiance. Of course, it would be hard to think of ways to be defiant like Mordecai every single day, but even Mordecai (or Polycarp, as I've already mentioned) was not defiant in precisely the same way every day of his life. I have no doubt that he lived a life of defiance against the evil forces around him, but only rarely was he presented an opportunity for the dramatic action he took as recounted in Esther 3. When the opportunity arrived, he was ready because of the many acts of quiet defiance he had taken throughout his life.

We train ourselves for the dramatic moments by the choices we make everyday. Dischal Sooku trained in martial arts, so that when a time came to offer help, he was ready. (Google it.) A soldier has a reasonable expectation of how he will perform in battle because of the training to which he has committed himself. Same for an athlete. Same for a Christian. The book of Daniel provides an interesting example. In the first chapter, Daniel and his three friends arrive in Babylon and immediately enter the Babylonian acculturation program so that they can become useful officers in Nebuchadnezzar's court. These noble Jewish youths accept all the training in the Babylonian language and literature and culture, except for one element: their diet. They will not eat the sumptuous food and drink provided by the king. This decision probably does not stem from a desire to keep kosher; after all, there are no instructions for kosher wine in the Torah. I prefer to see this decision as an act of defiance, as if these Jewish boys are saying, "I will go this far, but no further." They will serve Nebuchadnezzar faithfully, but they will retain an aspect of their lives not given over to the Babylonians. In this way, they hold Babylonian culture at arm's length, training themselves for those moments—and those moments would come!—when they would need to make a more dramatic act of defiance.

If we want to be ready for the dramatic moments when a decisive act of defiance is necessary, we need to train ourselves by committing to quotidian acts of defiance. We need to follow Daniel's example by keeping the culture of Babylon at arm's length—not rejecting all elements of the culture around us, but not wholeheartedly embracing everything, either. Jesus tells a parable about some seed that when thrown falls on different types of ground (Mark 4:1–9). "And some fell among thorns, and the thorns grew up, and choked it, and it yielded no fruit" (4:7). Jesus tells us that these thorns represent "the cares of this world, and the deceitfulness of riches, and the lusts of other things," and that the effect of these thorns is that they "choke the word, and it becometh unfruitful" (4:19). Jesus is telling us specific ways in which we need to hold the culture of Babylon at arm's length in quotidian acts of defiance. Our everyday defiance should involve "the cares of this world" (perhaps abstaining from social media? perhaps politics?), "the deceitfulness of riches" (perhaps turning down a promotion? perhaps resisting the impulse of hoarding?), and "the lusts of other things" (think: mid-life crisis and all that it entails). It's not that all of these things are sinful *per se*, but being completely enmeshed in the culture of Babylon chokes the word so that it yields nothing. There may be a nice-looking plant that appears healthy, but—like the fig tree (Mark 11:13)—there is no fruit. (Most summers I've got some tomato plants like this; very frustrating!) Quotidian defiance should not be all negative, though, but should also involve the spiritual disciplines of prayer and Bible reading and other edifying actions that separate us from the culture of the world (cf. Rom 12:2).

***

One of the main themes of Richard Hughes' history of churches of Christ is the transition from sectarianism to denominationalism.[11] The way Hughes uses this terminology, "sectarianism" means a posture directed against the culture of the world and toward the kingdom of God (it's a good thing), whereas "denominationalism" is the opposite, a comfort with the culture of the world, a desire to fit in. Hughes accuses churches of Christ in the twentieth century of moving from sectarianism to denominationalism, from a posture opposing the culture of the world to a posture embedded within that culture. No matter what you think of

Hughes' historical narrative or even his use of this terminology, it is worth reflecting based on your experience whether this particular accusation holds any merit. Have churches of Christ grown too comfortable in the culture of Babylon?

If we want to follow Mordecai's example, it's not just gonna happen. If we don't heed the advice of Jesus in the Parable of the Sower, if we don't follow the example of Daniel and his friends, then when the dramatic moment arrives that requires decisive action, we will find that we have no desire to rock the boat by standing when everyone else is kneeling before Haman.

Brethren, let us prepare for our moment of testing—when perhaps we will stand alone against the evil forces and face severe repercussions for doing so, hoping in the promise of the crown of life (Rev 2:10)—by making the daily determination to defy the weed-loving culture of Babylon so that we may bear fruit for God.

Endnotes

1. This chapter first appeared in *For Such a Time as This: Restoring God's People in Ezra, Nehemiah, and Esther*, ed. Doug Burleson (Henderson, TN: FHU Press, 2023). Used by permission. I appreciate Clay McFerrin's close reading of this essay and his helpful comments.

[2] Carl R. Trueman, *Strange New World: How Thinkers and Activists Redefined Identity and Sparked the Sexual Revolution* (Wheaton, IL: Crossway, 2022), 115.

[3] The Greek version of Esther promotes this interpretation in the additional passage known as Esther 13:12–14 (= C 5–7). See also the way Jesus quotes Deuteronomy 6:13 at Matthew 4:10; Luke 4:8. If Mordecai's objection centered

on the practice rather than the person of Haman, he was not unique in his stance; see Amélie Kuhrt, *The Persian Empire: A Corpus of Sources from the Achaemenid Period* (London: Routledge, 2007), 534–39.

[4] See Paul Hartog, *Polycarp's Epistle to the Philippians and the Martyrdom of Polycarp: Introduction, Text, and Commentary* (Oxford: Oxford University Press, 2013).

[5] Translation in Michael W. Holmes, ed., *The Apostolic Fathers: Greek Texts and English Translations*, 3d ed (Grand Rapids: Baker, 2007), 315.

[6] On this accusation against the early Christians (and Jews), see Larry W. Hurtado, *Destroyer of the Gods: Early Christian Distinctiveness in the Roman World* (Waco: Baylor University Press, 2016), 56–57, but also the wider discussion (52–62). Hurtado summarizes: "the radical selectivity and exclusivity of early Christian worship was neither acceptable nor even readily comprehensible to the wider Roman-era public" (57).

[7] For a picture of such a token, see Douglas A. Foster, *A Life of Alexander Campbell* (Grand Rapids: Eerdmans, 2020), 40–42. The same sort of token was required for the communion service during the famous Cane Ridge revival; see C. Leonard Allen, *Distant Voices: Discovering a Forgotten Past for a Changing Church* (Abilene: ACU Press, 1993), ch. 2, esp. p. 10.

[8] Thomas W. Grafton, *Alexander Campbell: Leader of the Great Reformation of the Nineteenth Century* (St. Louis: Christian Publishing Company, 1897), 40–41.

[9] Earl Irvin West, *The Search for the Ancient Order: A History of the Restoration Movement 1849–1950*, vol. 1 (Indianapolis: Religious Book Service, 1949), 52.

[10] Robert Richardson, *Memoirs of Alexander Campbell,*

2 vols (Philadelphia: J. B. Lippincott & Co., 1868–1870), 1.190.

[11] Richard T. Hughes, *Reviving the Ancient Faith: The Story of Churches of Christ in America* (Grand Rapids: Eerdmans, 1996).

Chapter 4

The Challenge of Love
Approaching Hosea[1]

H osea lived in the eighth century BC, according to the first verse of the book. The kings named there all reigned between about 750–700 BC. That dating makes Hosea more-or-less a contemporary of a few other prophets: Amos, Micah, and Isaiah name some of the same kings in the first verses of their books, and Jonah also lived at this same time (cf. 2 Kgs 14:25). But Hosea is unique among this group of prophets; in fact, he's unique among all prophets, because he's the only northern prophet for whom we have a book of oracles. Remember that after the death of Solomon, the kingdom of Israel split in two (cf. 1 Kgs 12), into a northern kingdom called Israel and a southern kingdom called Judah. Almost all the prophets who have books named after them are from the south, the nation of Judah. That's true of Isaiah, Amos, Micah, and most of the others. Jonah is from the north (again, see 2 Kgs 14:25), but we don't have a book of Jonah's oracles, we just have a story about Jonah (with one, very brief oracle; Jonah 3:4). Amos, like Hosea, did prophesy to the northern nation of Israel, but Amos was actually from the south (see Amos 1:1; 7:12–15). So the book of Hosea—alone among all the books of the Bible—preserves for us a collection of oracles from a northern prophet.

As soon as Jeroboam the son of Nebat founded the northern nation of Israel, he established a state-sponsored religion centered around veneration of golden cows, one in Dan in the far north, another in Bethel close to the border with Judah (1 Kgs 12:26–33). As in the case of the golden cow that Aaron made for the people at Sinai (Exod 32:1–6), these cows in Dan and Bethel were probably supposed to be idols of Yahweh, Israel's God.[2] Jeroboam identifies the cow as representing the one "who brought you up from the land of Egypt" (1 Kgs 12:28; cf. Exod 32:4). This sin of worshiping Yahweh through an idol defiled the northern nation of Israel throughout their history. At their best, the northerners were idolaters.

When Ahab came to the throne of Israel, things got worse.

> Then, as if following the sin of Jeroboam son of Nebat were not enough, he married Jezebel, the daughter of Ethbaal king of the Sidonians, and then proceeded to serve Baal and bow in worship to him (1 Kgs 16:31).

No longer were they idolaters; now they were pagans, worshiping foreign gods. You remember Elijah's contest on Mt. Carmel with the prophets of Baal (1 Kgs 18), and the Lord's words that there were 7000 (only!) who had not bowed the knee to Baal (19:18).

A century later, in the days of a second Jeroboam—this one, the son of Jehoash (cf. 2 Kgs 14:23–29)—the situation was largely the same, as we see in Hosea.

Marrying Gomer

God called Hosea to do something pretty strange, something that we would never advise our own children to do. God told Hosea to go find himself an unfaithful woman and marry her (1:2). Of course, when God gives these strange commands—such as telling Isaiah to walk around naked (Isa 20) or telling Ezekiel to lie on his side for more than a year (Ezek 4)—he does so in order to prove a point. Hosea's marriage with Gomer, the unfaithful woman, will provide a living demonstration of what God's relationship with Israel is like.

Israel is the unfaithful woman.

> Yes, their mother is promiscuous; she conceived them and acted shamefully. For she thought, "I will follow my lovers, the men who give me my food and water, my wool and flax, my oil and drink" (2:5).

The entire book of Hosea is a meditation on the unfaithfulness of Israel. Chapter 4 details sin after sin. The problem is, of course, that they worship Baal, but also that they worship that cow in Bethel (which Hosea derisively calls Beth-aven, "house of sin," rather than Bethel, "house of God"; 4:15). The problem is the priests, who do not teach (4:4), and the prophets, who prophesy lies (4:5). "My people are destroyed for lack of knowledge" (4:6).

> My people consult their wooden idols, and their divining rods inform them. For a spirit of promiscuity leads them astray; they act promiscuously in disobedience to their God (4:12).

At this point, we could talk about the evils of idolatry, and how idolatry still affects modern western Christians, though in different and perhaps less obvious ways than it affected ancient Israelites. We could take some time to talk about our relationship to money, or our obsession with entertainment, or social media, or our jobs, or having the perfect family, or any number of things that are not God. We need to hear these lessons, and the book of Hosea wants to tell us about our sin. It wants us to see ourselves in the role of Gomer, the unfaithful spouse, abandoning our one true love for what cannot possibly satisfy. The book of Hosea is a meditation on the unfaithfulness of God's people.

But the book of Hosea, even more so, is a meditation on the love of God. Hosea the prophet is an image of God. What God wants to communicate through this marriage of the prophet and the harlot is not only how unfaithful Israel has been, but how much pain Israel's unfaithfulness has caused God—pain caused by God's deep love for his people.

Hear God, the wounded lover, speak about his dear one.

> *She does not recognize*
> *that it is I who gave her the grain,*
> *the new wine, and the fresh oil.*
> *I lavished silver and gold on her,*
> *which they used for Baal (2:8).*

> *Therefore, I am going to persuade her,*
> *lead her to the wilderness and speak tenderly*
> *to her (2:14).*

God wants to take Israel back to the beginning of their relationship, where they went on their first date, in a manner of speaking. God is angry and hurt, but even more so he longs for the relationship to be restored. He just wants his people back. So he will court his wife again. Once he gets Israel back to the wilderness, God has it all planned out.

> *There I will give her vineyards back to her*
> *and make the Valley of Achor into a gateway*
> *   of hope.*
> *There she will respond as she did in the days*
> *   of her youth,*
> *as in the day she came out of the land of*
> *   Egypt.*
> *In that day, says the Lord,*
> *you will call me "My husband" and no longer*
> *   "My baal."*
> *For I will remove the names of the Baals from*
> *   her mouth;*
> *they will no longer be remembered by their*
> *   names* (2:15–17).

Even though *baal* is sometimes just a Hebrew word meaning "husband," God said he didn't want Israel using that word anymore, because it sounds too much like Israel's ex-boyfriend. What God wants more than anything is not to punish Israel but to love Israel and be loved in return.

The image of a marriage is not the only image Hosea uses to depict God's relationship with Israel. Another way of looking at it is that God is Israel's father, and Israel is the disobedient son.

> *When Israel was a child I loved him,*
> *and out of Egypt I called my son* (11:1).

God is the tender-hearted father who lavishes gifts on his child.

> *It was I who taught Ephraim to walk,*
> *taking them by the hand,*
> *but they never knew that I healed them.*
> *I led them with human cords,*
> *with ropes of love.*
> *To them I was like one who eases the yoke*
>   *from their jaws;*
> *I bent down to give them food* (11:3–4).

But Israel is so disobedient, God decides to punish his son (11:2, 6–7). Then the unexpected happens—God has a change of heart. He cannot give up on his beloved son, which leads to "an utterance whose daring is unparalleled in the whole of prophecy."[3]

> *How can I give you up, Ephraim?*
> *How can I surrender you, Israel?*
> *How can I make you like Admah?*
> *How can I treat you like Zeboiim? I*
> *have had a change of heart; my compassion is*
>   *stirred!*
> *I will not vent the full fury of my anger;*
> *I will not turn back to destroy Ephraim.*
> *For I am God and not man, the Holy One*
>   *among you;*
> *I will not come in rage* (11:8–9).

God is like the father in the Parable of the Prodigal Son. (In fact, God is the father in the Parable of the Prodigal Son.)

The younger son abandons his family and burns through his inheritance doing all the things his father had warned him about. And when this prodigal son decides to return home, there is his father, standing at the edge of their property, peering into the horizon on the lookout for his boy (Luke 15:20). Sure, there had no doubt been moments when this father had been angry with his son, had thought to himself, "If I ever see that boy again, why I'll...." But when it came right down to it, the father just wanted a relationship with his son. When the boy came back, the father felt no bitterness, just delight.

The Call of God

God calls on Hosea to be an image of God. God calls on his servants to be an image of God. And in the case of the book of Hosea, God is the wounded lover, the hurting father, longing for relationship with his people. He calls on us to do the same. God calls on his people to love at the risk of a broken heart.

In the movie *Room* (2015), a mom has to convince her small son to help her escape from their abductor, so she tells him a story, explaining things he doesn't understand. At one point, this boy looks up at his mom and yells, "I want a different story!" and the mom yells back, "No! This is the story that you get!"[4]

There are many times that we'd like a different story. Right after Peter had confessed Jesus as the Messiah, and then Jesus started to explain about his impending death— teaching for which Peter was not at all ready—Peter essentially looked at Jesus and said, "I want a different story" (cf. Mark 8:27–33). But Jesus had to tell Peter, "No, this is the story that you get." I bet Paul sometimes wished he didn't have to endure all these hardships in order to bring salvation to the world (2 Cor 11:24–29). But that is the story that God had prepared for Paul (Acts 9:16).

I can imagine Hosea looking up to heaven and saying, "I want a different story. I don't want to marry this unfaithful woman. I don't want to go find her again. It hurts too much." And God responds, "No, Hosea, this is the story that you get. You have been called to image me. And that means you must love even when it hurts, because that's who I am."

Followers of Christ love others even when it hurts. There are times in our families that it gets hard to love people, but we will love them even when it hurts. It gets hard in church sometimes to love fellow Christians, but if we are going to imitate God, we will love people even when it hurts.

When my wife and I first decided to get involved in foster care, one older member of our church who had fostered children decades earlier told me, "Prepare to have your heart broken." He meant that foster parents take in kids who have been in some pretty rough situations, and the foster kids become a part of this new family. Foster parents provide for these kids, and support them, attend their school functions and their sporting events; foster parents love their foster kids. And then, usually, after a while, a state agent comes and removes the children from the foster home and puts them back in a situation that is—shall we say?—less than ideal. And it breaks your heart. So, what? Should you not love these kids at all? That is no kind of solution for people who imitate God, because our God loves even when it hurts.

***

What is the message of Hosea? Paul sums it up well.

So be imitators of God, as beloved children, and live in love, as Christ loved us and handed himself over for us as a sacrificial offering to God for a fragrant aroma (Eph 5:1–2).

Hosea is a vision of grace, because he is an image of our God.

Endnotes

[1] This chapter first appeared in *Visions of Grace: Stories from Scripture*, Berean Study Series, ed. Ed Gallagher (Florence, AL: Heritage Christian University Press, 2019).

[2] For more about these cows, see the next chapter, on Amos.

[3] Gerhard von Rad, *Old Testament Theology*, 2 vols. (New York: Harper & Row, 1965), 2.145.

[4] You can see the scene on YouTube; search "Room I want a different story."

Chapter 5

Does Amos Condemn All Sacrifice?
Approaching Amos 5[1]

About the middle of the eighth century BC, a shepherd named Amos left his home in the small Judean town of Tekoa, south of Bethlehem (Amos 1:1). He headed to Bethel (cf. Amos 7:10–17), a town in the bordering nation of Israel whose first king, Jeroboam I, had established a sanctuary there for a golden bull representing Yahweh (1 Kgs 12:28–29), the national deity of both Judah and Israel.[2] Upon arriving, this shepherd-turned-prophet boldly announced God's judgment upon Israel, culminating in exile (Amos 4:2–3; 5:5; 6:7–14; 7:17), for sins surpassing even those of her neighbors Aram, Edom, Judah, and others (cf. Amos 1–2). Israel's guilt centered on the callousness of her people in the face of the poor and suffering in her own land (4:1; 5:11–12; 8:4–6), which directly contradicted not only the laws established by Yahweh (cf. Exod 22:21–27) but also the example of Yahweh himself (cf. Amos 2:6–16). But more surprising was Amos' declarations that even the altars of Bethel, which surely were conceived by the Israelites as a means of obtaining Yahweh's favor, would be destroyed on the day of Israel's punishment (3:14; 5:5; cf. 7:9). In fact, Amos uniformly expresses a negative evaluation of the Bethel sanctuary, proclaiming that the sacrifices themselves constituted sin (4:4–5) and that they elicit Yahweh's disgust:

> I hate, I reject your festivals, nor do I delight in your solemn assemblies. Even though you offer up to me burnt offerings and your grain offerings, I will not accept them; and I will not even look at the peace offerings of your fatlings. Take away from me the noise of your songs; I will not even listen to the sound of your harps. But let justice roll down like waters and righteousness like an ever-flowing stream (5:21–24).

We might seek an explanation for these sentiments from the blasphemous nature of the worship at Bethel. After all, the Bible consistently depicts the erection of the bovine icons in two northern cities of Dan and Bethel as the great sin of the newly-created nation of Israel (as distinct from Judah, its southern neighbor) following the death of Solomon (see 1 Kgs 12:30; cf. 15:30; etc.). Not only does the representation of Yahweh by an idol contradict the second commandment (Exod 20:4–6; Deut 5:8–10; cf. 4:9–20),[3] but the location of these new shrines in the North deters the people from traveling to the divinely-ordained place of worship in Jerusalem (cf. Deut 12), which in fact was Jeroboam's express purpose in founding these two northern sanctuaries (1 Kgs 12:26–28). The priests who ministered at these sites usually could not claim a genealogy appropriate to their office (cf. 1 Kgs 12:31). Moreover, Amos describes the nature of the sacrifices as antithetical to the laws ordained at Sinai (5:5) in that they contain leaven (cf. Lev 2:11) and those offering freewill sacrifices boast of what should be a private matter (cf. Matt 6:1–4).

If we are on the right track in explaining Amos' harsh attitude toward the sacrificial cult in terms of the illegitimate rites practiced especially at the northern sanctuaries, we may look for parallels in Hosea, the only other canonical prophet whose oracles are directed toward the North. Indeed, we do find there similar sentiments.

> He has rejected your calf, O Samaria, saying, "My anger burns against them!" How long will they be incapable of innocence? For from Israel is even this! A craftsman made it, so it is not God; surely the calf of Samaria will be broken to pieces (Hos 8:5–6).

Clearly, Hosea finds the worship involving the golden calf and its "idolatrous priests" (10:5) to be deplorable (cf. 13:2). The obvious difference between Hosea and Amos, who were rough contemporaries in time and location (cf. Hos 1:1; Amos 1:1), is that Hosea makes his condemnation of illicit worship so much more explicit. He condemned not only worship of the calf as a representation of Yahweh, but also the syncretism that combined worship of Yahweh with the Canaanite god Baal (Hos 1–3). In this way, Hosea rightly reminds us of the northern prophet Elijah in his struggles a century earlier to thwart the syncrestic religious policies of Ahab and Jezebel, those monarchs who more than any other were responsible for promoting the worship of Baal in Israel (1 Kgs 17–18).

However, two reasons compel us to search further for the motivation for Amos' condemnation of sacrifice in 5:21–24. First, Amos himself never so much as mentions Baal or even the golden calf worshiped in Bethel, though he did quarrel with its priest, Amaziah (Amos 7:10–17); therefore, such practices could form only a part of the background for his words in 5:21–24. Second, the concept of God's opposition to sacrifice appears not infrequently in other parts of scripture which must have in view the legitimate practices at the Jerusalem Temple. Prominent among these is the conclusion to Psalm 51:

> For you do not delight in sacrifice, otherwise I
>   would give it;
> you are not pleased with burnt offering.
> The sacrifices of God are a broken spirit;
> a broken and a contrite heart, O God, You
>   will not despise (51:16–17; cf. 40:6; Heb
>   10:5–7).

Similarly, Isaiah condemns the sacrifices offered by the Judeans at the Temple:

> What are your multiplied sacrifices to me?
> says the Lord.
> I have had enough of burnt offerings of rams
>   and the fat of fed cattle;
> and I take no pleasure in the blood of bulls,
>   lambs or goats (Isa 1:11).

Any satisfactory explanation for Amos' judgment against sacrifice must also encompass the analogous statements by Isaiah and the Psalmist.

Some commentators have assumed that the prophets opposed on principle the ritual associated with sacrifice.[4]

George Buchanan Gray, in his commentary on Isaiah, presented a rather tame version of this view:

> It is not necessary to conclude that Isaiah regarded sacrifice as positively offensive and intolerable to God under all conditions, but he regards it as something that Yahweh does not require, and that in no way palliates the sin of those who offer it.[5]

Nevertheless, the clear and consistent message of Israel's scriptures depicts sacrifice as not only approved but commanded by God. It is true that the Bible does not specify who initiated the idea of sacrifice, whether God or man. Concerning the first pair of sacrifices recorded in the Bible, we are told neither the criteria for securing divine favor by sacrifice nor the motivation prompting Cain and Abel to bring their offerings in the first place (Gen 4:3–5).[6] In any case, we soon notice that sacrifice features prominently in man's relationship with God, as Noah presents burnt offerings (Gen 8:20), while Abraham (12:7; etc.), Isaac (26:25), and Jacob (33:20) construct altars to God, and Jacob, at least, offers sacrifices (31:54; 46:1). In the Exodus Story, God demands that Pharaoh release the Israelites specifically so that they might sacrifice to him in the wilderness (Exod 3:18; 5:3; etc.). In preparation for the Tenth Plague, God instituted the Passover ordinance, which includes the sacrifice of a lamb (12:3–10; cf. 12:27), and immediately after the exodus he intimated that sacrifice would become a major part of true Israelite religion (13:11–15). Moses' father-in-law Jethro, the priest of Midian (cf. 2:16–21, where he is called Reuel), offered sacrifices when visiting the Israelite camp (18:12). Finally, in the covenant at Sinai God intro-

duced detailed regulations regarding sacrifice (20:24; 23:18–
19; cf. Lev 1–7), which had to be obeyed precisely (cf. Lev
10:1–2), and the people responded with sacrifice (Exod 24:5;
contrast Amos 5:25; Jer 7:22).

And yet, as important as sacrifice was in Israelite religion, the Bible frequently downplays its significance in the
light of what Jesus would call "the weightier provisions of
the law" (Matt 23:23). For, though the Historical Books
often depict in a positive manner early Israel offering sacrifices on various altars in their new homeland (e.g., Josh 8:31;
Judg 2:5; 1 Sam 1:3), King Saul's two major acts of disobedience both involve an improper focus on sacrifice (1 Sam
13:8–14; 15:20–21). In the second of these episodes, the
king admitted to allowing the people to reserve some of the
spoil of Amalek (all of which was to be devoted to destruction; cf. 15:2–3) so that they might sacrifice it (15:21).
Samuel's response properly contextualizes such pseudo-
piety: "Has the Lord as much delight in burnt offerings and
sacrifices as in obeying the voice of the Lord? Behold, to obey
is better than sacrifice, and to heed than the fat of rams"
(15:22).

The prophets document the perversion of Israelite
worship in terms of the improper motivations from the
participants. The religious leadership (priests and prophets)
often performed their duties simply for the paycheck (cf. Mic
3:5, 11) so that they often gave little attention to the spiritual
aspects of their office (cf. Isa 28:7). Since Micah and Isaiah
describe the situation as it pertains to Judah in the second
half of the eighth century BC, Amos was probably dealing
with similar problems a few decades earlier in Israel. Indeed,
Hosea confirms that the northern priests at this time had
"rejected knowledge," would not teach the divine statutes

(4:6), and behaved in such a manner that they resembled murderers (6:9). The people themselves followed the example of their leaders (cf. Hos 4:9) and no doubt thought similarly that God was with them (cf. Mic 3:11) even as they engaged in idolatrous practices (Hos 4:11–14). The main point is once again sounded by Hosea: "For I delight in loyalty rather than sacrifice, and in the knowledge of God rather than burnt offerings" (6:6).

With this distortion of true worship in view, we may look again at Isaiah's condemnation of sacrifice. He goes on to say:

> *Bring your worthless offerings no longer,*
> *incense is an abomination to me.*
> *New moon and sabbath, the calling of*
>   *assemblies—*
> *I cannot endure iniquity and the solemn*
>   *assembly.* [...]
> *Wash yourselves, make yourselves clean;*
> *remove the evil of your deeds from my sight.*
> *Cease to do evil,*
> *learn to do good;*
> *seek justice,*
> *reprove the ruthless,*
> *defend the orphan,*
> *plead for the widow* (Isa 1:13, 16–17).

Isaiah's emphasis on the need for pure hearts as demonstrated through compassionate and righteous lives as a prerequisite to acceptable worship coheres not only with Amos' message (cf. 2:7; 4:1; 5:10–15) but also that of Micah (6:6-8), Jeremiah (7:9–11), the Psalmist (24:3–4), and our Lord (Matt 5:23–24).

The problem that Amos addresses in 5:21–24 involves the mindset that the rituals commanded by God are disconnected from the lifestyles of his people. Amos' audience assumed that the efficacy of their worship lay in their technical adherence to certain details; having thus completed the required ceremony, the people had successfully obtained God's favor and could continue in their lives unconcerned about any particular moral responsibilities. The Israelites had accepted the lie propagated by the worshippers of Baal and other gods that sacrifice was an effective means of manipulating deities into providing certain blessings (e.g., a good harvest), and that the gods issued no ethical demands (cf. Mic 3:11; Zeph 1:12). Amos declares that when Yahweh receives sacrifices accompanied by such an attitude, he hates and rejects them. As Jeremias says,

> without 'justice and righteousness' (v. 24) there is no possibility for contact between Israel and God to begin with. Israel celebrates Yahweh as if its relationship with God were intact, utterly unaware that he is not even present at the celebration.[7]

It is unnecessary to belabor the point that the words of Amos retain their relevance for Christians in the twenty-first century. We must remember today that "pure and undefiled religion" (Jas 1:27) starts outside the church building with "justice" and "righteousness" (Amos 5:24).

Endnotes

[1] This essay first appeared in *Proclamation and Promise: Major Themes in the Minor Prophets. The 75th Annual*

Freed-Hardeman University Lectureship, ed. David L. Lipe (Henderson, TN.: Freed-Hardeman University, 2011), 212–17. Used by Permission.

[2] On the bull iconography, see Richard S. Hess, *Israelite Religions: An Archaeological and Biblical Survey* (Grand Rapids: Baker, 2007), 158 n. 47.

[3] For discussion, see Hess, *Israelite Religions*, 165–66.

[4] For discussion and rejection of this idea, see Jörg Jeremias, *The Book of Amos: A Commentary*, Old Testament Library (Louisville: WJK, 1998), 101–7.

[5] George Buchanan Gray, *A Critical and Exegetical Commentary on the Book of Isaiah*, 2 vols., International Critical Commentary (Edinburgh: T&T Clark, 1912), 1.xc.

[6] See Hess, *Israelite Religions*, 179–80.

[7] Jeremias, *Book of Amos*, 103.

Section 2

The New Testament

Chapter 6

The Bible Is Our Blueprint
Approaching Luke 4:1–13

For the word of God is living and powerful, and sharper than any two-edged sword, piercing even to the division of soul and spirit, and of joints and marrow, and is a discerner of the thoughts and intents of the heart (Heb 4:12).

For we do not have a High Priest who cannot sympathize with our weaknesses, but was in all points tempted as we are, yet without sin (Heb 4:15).

I know a business that, decades ago, hired an architect to draw some plans for a new building. This business wanted to dream about possibilities for the future, and they wanted a drawing to help them imagine that future. The drawing hung in a room of the business for several years until it became clear that this imagined new building was only a dream; it would never be a reality. While it was hanging on the wall, we could have entered that room and seen the plans, remembering what the architect had imagined. But the plans were never enacted. It was just an idea.

When it comes to buildings, it is usually fine for the plans never to come to fruition. But there are areas in our lives when the plans really need to be enacted, when just imagining the plans is not nearly good enough. The town in which I live recently installed a roundabout at one of the traffic intersections. We don't have many roundabouts around here. I've been to other countries where roundabouts are much more common, but where I live it took people a while to get used to the traffic flow. When I first happened upon it, I was very confused and nearly turned the wrong way. If other cars had been present, that could have spelled disaster.

Scripture: Our Living Blueprint

There are several ways in which the analogy of Scripture to a Christian blueprint is helpful. But before even getting to those similarities, let's notice one thing right away: Scripture must be enacted. Sometimes we might be tempted to treat Scripture like that business I mentioned treated its architectural plans: put it up on the wall, look at it every once in a while, and imagine what life would be like if we put it into practice. After all, the life that Scripture imagines for followers of Jesus might seem like a dream, like something almost impossible to accomplish. Oh, sure, there are some things that are relatively easy to accomplish, that we do quite readily: we'll get baptized, we'll attend worship services, we'll try to remember to pray and read our Bibles. Certainly, those are things we ought to do.

What about the weightier matters of the law? Remember

how Jesus identified those weightier matters? That would be justice and mercy and faithfulness (Matt 23:23). What about all the things He talks about in the Sermon on the Mount, things like avoiding anger and lust (Matt 5:21–30), turning the other cheek (5:38–42), refusing to worry (6:25–34), or treating others the way we wish we were treated (7:12)? These are the types of things we like to hang on the wall and look at every so often. Jesus seems to think that His followers won't just look at His plans for the building but will actually build it.

Let's remind ourselves of what Scripture says about Scripture. According to Paul, the fact that Scripture is inspired by God means that it is "profitable for doctrine, for reproof, for correction, for instruction in righteousness" (2 Tim 3:16). Scripture is useful, profitable, to us, not to look at but to live. We need to allow Scripture to do its work on our lives, to train us in righteousness.

It's not going to be easy. Scripture presents a vision of life that is hard. Jesus called it the narrow and difficult way that few people find (Matt 7:13–14). It's going to hurt to follow the way of Jesus. We should always remember that His way leads to a cross, and He calls others to join Him in bearing a cross (Luke 9:23; 14:27). The writer of Hebrews says that Scripture is living and powerful, and like a sharp sword it will determine the thoughts and intentions of our heart (Heb 4:12). If we will commit ourselves to living out Scripture, to not just hanging it up on the wall but to build the life it imagines, it will not allow us to be satisfied with what good Christians we are. We will identify with the tax collector more than the Pharisee (Luke 18:9–14). If that's not how we see ourselves, it's probably because we've hung

Scripture on the wall and have ceased attempting to put it into practice.

There's no doubt we will fail to live fully the life Scripture presents. That's why we have a Savior. And this Savior gave an example of how to allow Scripture to govern your life.

The Temptation of Jesus

Immediately after His baptism (Luke 3:21–22), Jesus was led by the Holy Spirit into the wilderness, where He would fast and face temptation from the devil. The Gospel of Mark merely mentions this period but does not tell the story (Mark 1:12–13). Both Matthew (4:1–11) and Luke (4:1–13) narrate the three temptations Jesus faced. Here we will focus on Luke's account.

The reason we're looking at the Temptation Narrative in a chapter on Scripture as the Christian blueprint is because of the way Jesus responds to the Satanic temptations. Each time He answers with Scripture. He provides an example of how Scripture trains us in righteousness. Moreover, inasmuch as Jesus refuses to do things we humans often fail to refuse to do, He provides an example of how Scripture can train us to follow the difficult way of Jesus.

The First Temptation

The devil told Jesus to use His divine power to turn stones into bread (Luke 4:3). (It's interesting that throughout the Gospels, while humans struggle to understand who Jesus is, the demons know full well who He is and where He came from.) Jesus had been fasting for forty days (4:2), so we might well imagine how tempting it would be to submit to the devil's suggestion.

How long have you gone without food before? Food is so plentiful in America, so easy to come by—you don't even have to cook it!—that most of us don't go but a few hours without having something in our mouths. But sometimes, for whatever reason, we experience some hunger. Maybe work or family responsibilities take so much of our attention that we have to skip some meals. Some of us might even choose to fast for a period of time. I myself have fasted a few times in my life, and I will say I don't like it. I do not enjoy depriving myself of food. I like eating. I've certainly never tried to fast for as long as Jesus did, so, again, it's easy to think how much Jesus would want that bread.

What's not so easy to see is why Jesus would consider it sinful to turn stones into bread. After all, such an action is never condemned in the Bible. Later, when Jesus feeds the five thousand (Luke 9:10–17), He takes a few fish and loaves of bread and multiplies them. Was it sinful for Him to multiply this food, essentially creating food where there had been no food? Of course not. Would it have been sinful for Jesus to turn stones into bread? Apparently so. This is one of those instances where it would have been nice if the Bible had provided us with more information. Why would this action be sinful? I'm not sure, but I have a suggestion.

My guess is that it would not always be sinful to turn stones into bread, but in certain situations it would be sinful, and Jesus was in one of those situations. Notice that He quotes Deuteronomy 8:3, where Moses tells the Israelites who had been in the wilderness:

So He humbled you, allowed you to hunger, and fed you
with manna which you did not know nor did your fathers
know, that He might make you know that man shall not
live by bread alone; but man lives by every word that
proceeds from the mouth of the Lord.

This is hard to hear. God wanted to train the Israelites to
trust Him, so He gave them hunger. Then He gave them
manna, but they couldn't collect as much manna as they
wanted; they could only gather as much as they needed for
one day, and they had to trust that there would be more
manna the next day (Exod 16:4). In this way, God trained
the Israelites out in the desert, before their entry into the
Promised Land, to understand that a person doesn't live only
on bread but on the word of God.

Jesus is out in the desert, like Israel, at the beginning of
his ministry, and He also has been given hunger from the
Lord. Remember it was the Holy Spirit who sent him into
the desert with no food. Did Jesus need training? I don't
know, but I do know that Luke 2:52 says that He grew in
wisdom and stature, and Hebrews 5:8 says that He learned
obedience through the things He suffered. I don't know if
Jesus needed training, but it seems like He's out in the desert
getting training just like the Israelites had been. And Jesus
interpreted His own experience as parallel to the experience
of Israel, as we know since He quoted this verse about their
wilderness wanderings. In that situation, yes, it would have
been sinful for Jesus to turn the stones into bread and
thereby forgo the training that God wanted to provide Him.
Jesus needed to rely on the word of God; He had before Him
things much more difficult even than a forty-day fast. Right

now, at the beginning of His ministry, He needed to commit to following the will of God wherever it led.

And it's Scripture that helped Him make that commitment and understand its stakes.

The Second Temptation

According to Luke, the second temptation involved the devil's offer to give Jesus all the kingdoms of the world in exchange for Jesus's worship of the devil. Such an action by Jesus would more clearly be a sin than would turning stones into bread, but just because the sin is obvious here should not lead us to diminish the strength of the temptation. (After all, Christians frequently fall prey to obvious sins.) The whole point of Jesus's ministry was to establish God's kingdom on earth (Luke 4:43), to create a community—which would come to be known as the church—dedicated to imitating Jesus and following the will of God. Jesus knew very well that it was going to take tremendous suffering on His part to bring about this kingdom (Luke 9:22; 17:25; 18:31–33). Avoiding suffering is one of our chief commitments; had we been in the place of Jesus, we would have thought of all kinds of justifications to succumb to this temptation. What if Jesus could establish a kingdom now, without any suffering? The devil is offering a pathway to an instant kingdom. (Does the devil have control of these kingdoms? He says that he has been given them, and elsewhere he is called "the ruler of the world," John 12:31.) If the foolish act of crucifixion (1 Cor 1:23) could accomplish the work of God, maybe God could use this foolish act instead, this bowing down to the devil. We can think of a way to trick the devil so that My bowing down to him really accomplishes his own destruction.

If Jesus had any such thoughts, Luke does not reveal them. Jesus is still thinking about Deuteronomy, and this time He quotes Deuteronomy 6:13 back at the devil. It's Scripture that fortifies Jesus against all temptation.

The Third Temptation

Finally, the devil tempts Jesus to display His power and control of God's angels, manifesting exactly how much authority He enjoys, an action that would surely fast-track people's belief in Him. The devil actually quotes Scripture at Jesus (Ps 91:11–12), but, of course, he is misusing it, a trick for which Jesus is fully prepared because of His own intense familiarity with Scripture. Once again, He quotes Deuteronomy (6:16 this time), and the devil departs "until an opportune time" (Luke 4:13). The devil will most certainly return, and we see later that he actually enters into one of Jesus's own disciples (22:3). Jesus is ready for the trial he will then face in part due to this early victory in reliance on Scripture.

***

Jesus used Scripture as His blueprint. Just read the rest of Luke's Gospel to see how often He quotes Scripture. He explains to people His own identity by reading to them Isaiah 61:1–2 (Luke 4:18–19). He explains the identity of John the Baptist by quoting Malachi 3:1 (Luke 7:27). He tells people why He's speaking in parables by quoting Isaiah 6:9 (Luke 8:10). He quotes Micah 7:6 in order to explain the nature of the choice he presents to people (Luke 12:53). After His resurrection, He opens people's minds to understand all the Scriptures and their relationship to Himself (Luke 24:27, 44–45).

If Scripture provided the blueprint for Jesus's life, surely we should use it in the same way. Like Jesus, we also need to understand our identity and the nature of this life we're living, and we need to understand it through the lens, or the plan, provided by Scripture. Of course, such a life is hard, seemingly impossible. Jesus says that in order to find our lives, we must lose them (Luke 9:24). Jesus found His life in Scripture, and we should do the same. Let's not just hang it on the wall; let's put it into practice.

Chapter 7

God Is Our Foundation

Approaching Matthew 7:24–27 // Luke 6:46–49[1]

Blessed are those who hear the word of God and keep it! (Luke 11:28)

I have done some stupid things in my life. Once at college, I was in a club that participated in a soapbox derby on campus, competing against other clubs. Somehow I got put in charge of our club's soapbox car one year, and somehow no one could find the car that had belonged to the club in previous years, or it had broke, or something. Anyway, I had to design a brand new car. That sort of thing would be a struggle for me now, but back in college, it wasn't just a challenge—it was quite impossible. The night before the race, I took a friend to a hardware store, where we purchased ... I don't know ... I think some ¾ inch plywood, some screws, and some wheels. We created a big, heavy box (not aerodynamic in the least), in which a man was supposed to ride down a hill—fast. Out of all our many failures, our biggest was the wheels, which were not secured to the vehicle well enough. I know, that sounds dangerous. But they weren't secured well enough even to be dangerous. As soon as our driver got in the car, the wheels popped off and the car just sat there on the road.

Let me say it again: that car had all kinds of problems—it was a long way from being a winner—but its biggest problem was the wheels, or, really, the way the wheels were attached to the frame. The wheels could not support the weight of the car and the driver. If the car had been perfect except for this one flaw, the result would have been the same. The car would not go.

Jesus tells a story about a couple fellows who both build houses, and both houses experienced the coming of a storm, but only one of the houses survived the storm. The difference, of course, was the foundation.

The Two Builders

The story of the wise and foolish builders appears twice in our Bibles, once at the end of the Sermon on the Mount (Matt 7:24–27) and again as the conclusion of Luke's Sermon on the Plain (Luke 6:46–49). This lesson will focus on the version in Luke with some attention to the version in Matthew. In both locations, the parable serves as the conclusion to a major block of teaching from Jesus.

Though less familiar, the version in Luke makes the same basic point as the version in Matthew and contains a little more detail as to the good builder's foundation. We all remember the kid's song, "The wise man built his house upon the rock," which is based on Matthew's version of the parable. Luke's version actually does not use the terms "wise man" and "foolish man," but one man still builds his house on rock (Greek *petra*). This man "dug deep and laid the foundation on the rock. And when the flood arose, the stream beat vehemently against that house, and could not shake it, for it was founded on the rock" (6:48). The other fellow built his house "on the earth without a foundation," so that when "the stream beat vehemently" against his house, "immediately it fell. And the ruin of that house was great" (6:49).

Where I live in northwest Alabama, we know something about the floods rising and houses being threatened by a stream—or, in our case, the Tennessee River. In recent years, we have had winters that set records for rainfall. A few years ago, the Tennessee River in our area rose to over thirty feet, whereas flood stage is at about eighteen feet. Our local newspaper ran stories about people with flooded homes who had no flood insurance because they didn't live close enough to the river to be in a designated flood zone. Even with all our sophisticated weather-prediction technology, floods have caught people off guard. It can happen fast. It can be unexpected.

Why would somebody be so dumb as to build a house without a foundation, as described in Jesus's parable? Well, let me remind you of my soapbox car. I built a piece of junk because (a) I didn't know what I was doing, and (b) I didn't have time to learn. Part of the issue here is time, and effort. Notice what the good builder does: "he dug deep and laid the foundation on the rock." Of course, that is the better thing to do, but it also takes time and energy. It's a lot easier to just start building right there on the ground rather than digging deep. Let's change the metaphor. Sometimes I'll cook a meal for my family, and I'll have to cut up some vegetables, perhaps potatoes, maybe an onion.

Anytime I do that, I have a little internal debate: "Do I want to spend a minute sharpening my knife? Maybe it's still sharp enough, since I did sharpen it before the last time I used it. But if it's not sharp enough, chopping vegetables is going to take longer. Plus, a dull knife is more dangerous than a sharp knife. If I end up cutting myself because I had to press harder on the dull knife, well, that's going to be a net loss. Better to just go ahead and sharpen the thing." Do you ever have debates with yourself like that? Sharpening a knife is a much different thing from building a house, but I can completely understand why someone might want to take the easy way out on some projects, cut some corners, save a little money, try to get done quicker.

There are a lot of times when we just want to take the easy way out. Do I want to put in the effort to be loving and respectful to my spouse? Do I want to invest in my kids right now, or just sit and read the paper or scroll through my feeds? I haven't read the Bible in a while, but I don't really get anything out of it, anyway. I should probably pray but I'm so tired.

Jesus is reminding us that the way of Jesus cannot be called "the easy way." It is a life of sacrifice, but it is also the only preparation for the coming storm.

The Coming Storm

Jesus reminds us in this parable that the storm is coming, and no matter how you might try, you cannot avoid the storm. The man who wisely builds his house on the rock still faces the storm and that vehemently-beating stream, just like the man who foolishly builds without a secure foundation. But you can prepare for the storm, and proper preparation will ensure that the storm doesn't wipe out your house.

What kind of storm is Jesus talking about? We use this metaphor so frequently that we probably hardly think about it in the context of this parable. We know exactly what "the storms of life" are. When you have marital problems, that is a stormy season. When you have rebellious teenagers, that's a storm. You go through a storm when you lose your job, or you get a bad diagnosis, or a family member dies. In all such situations, you will find help in the teachings of Jesus. If you base your life on Jesus, if God is your foundation, you will make it through these storms with your house intact.

I don't think so. I don't mean that I doubt that the teachings of Jesus can provide guidance and security through life's difficulties. I just don't think that's what Jesus is talking about. What would that interpretation of the parable even mean? What would the house represent, in that case? Let's say you're having marital problems, and you base your life on the teachings of Jesus, then ... what? The marital problems will go away? Is that what it means that the house survives the storm? But, no, we can't really believe that. You might end up getting a divorce. If your spouse wants to leave, basing your life on Jesus's teachings is not necessarily going to prevent it. So what does it mean that the house survives the storm? Maybe that you come through your marital problems with your faith intact? But that would basically mean that if you base your life on the teachings of Jesus, then you will base your life on the teachings of Jesus. Or, think of it from the other side: are we supposed to believe that someone without Jesus will face more difficulties in these storms? In what way would that be? Jesus actually tells His disciples that they are going to face difficulties in life specifically because they are His disciples (Luke 6:22–23). I don't think the storm represents life's difficulties.

The storm is judgment. The parable is not about troublesome times during our lives, but about the end of our lives. Jesus is trying to get us ready to face the final storm, the big one. The only way to survive it is to base our lives on His teachings. Failure to do so will ensure the destruction of our house.

Remember that Luke has already introduced us to the teachings of John the Baptist, who warned that "One mightier than I is coming" (3:16). "His winnowing fan is in His hand, and He will thoroughly clean out His threshing floor, and gather the wheat into His barn; but the chaff He will burn with unquenchable fire" (3:17). This is a description of "the wrath to come" (3:7).

The storm of God's judgment is coming. There's only one way to prepare. Listen to what Jesus says—and do it!

Hearing and Doing

> But be doers of the word, and not hearers only, deceiving yourselves. For if anyone is a hearer of the word and not a doer, he is like a man observing his natural face in a mirror; for he observes himself, goes away, and immediately forgets what kind of man he was. But he who looks into the perfect law of liberty and continues in it, and is not a forgetful hearer but a doer of the work, this one will be blessed in what he does (Jas 1:22–25).

The way Jesus tells it, the foolish builder is like a person who hears Jesus's words and does nothing about it (Luke 6:49).

The wise builder is like a person who hears Jesus's words and puts them into practice. The difference is not that one heard the word and the other did not. They both heard. The difference is that only one of them enacted Jesus's words.

Now, of course, hearing is necessary, and the fact that you are reading a book like this shows your commitment to hearing the words of Jesus. I wonder how committed you are to doing them. Please, don't take offence. I don't mean that you're so much worse at doing what Jesus says than I am. I mean that what Jesus asks us to do is hard, and it is easier said (or heard) than done. Remember the illustration from the previous chapter about the set of blueprints hanging on the wall, never enacted? That fits here, doesn't it? I remember watching cooking shows when I was younger, and my mouth would water as I saw those chefs create magnificent meals, but never once did I actually go in the kitchen and prepare their recipe, and so I never ate one of those meals. If you want to eat the meal, hearing about it is not enough; you've got to cook it.

Before getting off "hearing," let me just say: our churches need to recommit to hearing the word of God. If God is our foundation (according to the title of this chapter), then we need to make it a point of emphasis to listen to what He has to say. I know, there are parts of the Bible that are hard to understand. But, look, these days, with how easy it is to own a Bible, with how many freely available study tools there are online (my favorites: Wikipedia and Google Maps), there is very little excuse for us not to at least make the attempt to read—or, rather, study—the Bible every day. Remember, the wise builder "dug deep and laid the foundation on the rock." Making the personal commitment to daily Bible study will do more to strengthen the church than just about anything else. After all, God gave his people Scripture to train them in righteousness (2 Tim 3:16).

Such training demands putting it into practice, and that is what Jesus wanted to emphasize in His parable of the two builders. And, by the way, what I just said about how personal Bible study will strengthen the church— that's really true only if (let me say it once again: *only if*) we commit ourselves to putting into practice what we read. Jesus told this parable (whether in Matthew or Luke) after a major block of teaching material. So the most immediate application has to do with the very words He had just been telling people. When He says that the wise builder "hears My sayings and does them," He means the sayings that He had just spoken—stuff like "love your enemies" (Luke 6:27) and "turn the other cheek" (6:29) and the Golden Rule (6:31) and "judge not" (6:37) and "forgive" (6:37). This is the kind of thing that will see you through the coming storm, but you've got to put it into practice. Because if you don't ... well, don't say that Jesus didn't warn you.

***

God is our foundation. The word of God is our foundation. Hearing and doing the word of God is our foundation. These statements do not contradict; they are mutually reinforcing. Just as Jesus said, "If you love me, keep my commandments" (John 14:15), so also we could say that if God is our foundation, that means—at least, in part—that we must trust and obey Him. Of course, we do not earn salvation (Eph 2:8–9), and obedience has nothing to do with accumulating merit; it has everything to do with trusting Him. As

the brother of Jesus says, hearing without doing is demonic
(Jas 2:19).

Endnotes

[1] This chapter first appeared in *A Gentle and Quiet Spirit: A
Festschrift for Barbara Ann Dillon*. Heritage Legacy Series.
(Florence, AL: Heritage Christian University Press, 2023),
78–87.

Chapter 8

Using Your Talents
Approaching Matthew 25:14–30[1]

Every good thing given and every perfect gift is from above, coming down from the Father of lights, with whom there is no variation or shifting shadow (Jas 1:17).

Christians are a blessed people, and these blessings come from God. We acknowledge that God "has blessed us with every spiritual blessing in the heavenly places in Christ" (Eph 1:3). Those blessings surely include redemption from sin and hope for a glorious future. The apostles also talked about other sorts of spiritual gifts that their readers needed to use for the benefit of others (cf. 1 Pet 4:10; Rom 12:3, 6; etc.). Paul explains extensively that the distribution of various spiritual gifts among the Corinthian believers was not designed to exalt individual Christians but to build up the body through love (1 Cor 12–14). Similarly, the apostle explains in Ephesians 4:11–16 that different believers have different functions and abilities so that the whole church may benefit.

Besides all these tremendous spiritual blessings, God

also provides for our physical needs (cf. Matt 6:25–34). Indeed, American Christians in the twenty-first century can rightly claim that God has blessed us materially more than most people in world history could "ask or imagine" (cf. Eph 2:20). Perhaps followers of Christ have not reflected enough on what God intends for us to do with all this abundance of wealth. We may assume that he wants us to live comfortable lives, that the fact that we happened to be born in America as opposed to some other country with more primitive conditions was simply a lucky break on our part, or perhaps part of God's design to make life easy on us. Maybe we think of our wealth like the Corinthians thought about their spiritual powers: it's all for me.

The Parable of the Talents suggests a different interpretation.

Setting

Before his betrayal and crucifixion, Jesus spends time preparing his disciples for their life and ministry without his physical presence among them (Matt 24–25). He talks some about the destruction of Jerusalem that would occur in a few decades, and he talks about his own glorious return in judgment, his Second Coming. He repeatedly emphasizes that his disciples need to be ready for the coming judgment, because it will happen unexpectedly, like a thief in the night (24:42–44). They need to be faithful and responsible slaves who do their work diligently (24:45–51). They need to be like wise virgins who, with adequate oil for their lamps, are ready to meet the bridegroom (25:1–13). They need to be like the slaves who use their master's resources for his advantage rather than hide it in the ground (25:14–30).

The Parable of the Talents—in its literal meaning—has to do with money. A *talent* was a unit of weight, about 50–75 lbs. The value of a talent varied depending on what material it was—gold, silver, copper—but it was always an enormous sum of money. A talent of gold, for instance, would have been equivalent to about 6000 denarii, which was the standard day's wage for a laborer (cf. Matt 20:1–16).[2] In March 2023, fifty lbs. of gold would be worth around $1.5M (at $1902 per ounce), so we can imagine the slave receiving five talents to have about 7.5 million dollars at his disposal. A similar parable is found in Luke 19:11–27, the Parable of the Pounds, but this parable seems to have a different point, and the unit of currency is much smaller: a *mina* or 'pound' is about 100 denarii.

Interpretation

This parable is about using the gifts that God has provided. We often (correctly) think about this parable as an admonition to our use abilities, and this interpretation is helped along by the fact that the English word 'talent' happens to mean 'ability'. In fact, the English word 'talent' with this meaning originated in interpretations of this parable. Literally, the Greek word 'talent' referred to money, but the parable uses this word to symbolize whatever gifts the Christian might possess.

Jesus says that each of the slaves receives talents in accordance with their abilities (25:15), an idea that corresponds to other biblical teachings regarding spiritual gifts (1 Pet 4:10; Rom 12:6). This notion is a unique aspect of this parable that does not appear in the surrounding parables and teachings.

The first two slaves used their talents and profited by

them. Jesus does not directly make an application from this point, but we might imagine that he intended for his followers to understand that they should use their abilities and resources for the benefit of others. He teaches this lesson directly on many occasions.[3] These slaves are rewarded by a lofty commendation and admittance to their master's joy (25:21, 23).

The third slave hid his talent in the ground because he was afraid of the master (vv. 24–25). The master also accuses the slave of being lazy (25:26), though the slave may have described himself as cautious. His fear of making a mistake with his talent paralyzed him, but his inactivity—his laziness—infuriated the master and led to the worst kind of punishment (v. 30). It seems that the master would have been less angry if the slave had used the talent in some way, even if his business venture resulted in a less successful return than the other slaves, or possibly even a loss. "A previous parable implies that fearful inaction is unwarranted because God will forgive unwise action with his resources (18:23–25)."[4]

Application

This parable has significant application for the church today in two directions: faithfulness and diligence leads to great reward; fear and sloth leads to menacing punishment. These lessons are taught in any number of passages of Scripture. The distinctive element in this parable is the emphasis on the gifts given by God to each disciple in accordance with his or her ability, and the need for the disciple to put these gifts to use.

The Parable of the Talents implies that followers of Jesus—individually and collectively—need to identify the gifts given by their master and employ them. Many of us can identify wealth as one of the gifts given to us by God, and our master expects us to use this gift on behalf of others. Other gifts that we have might include various talents or opportunities; squandering them angers our master. Our children are gifts, and we must diligently and carefully mold them without wasting our opportunities. The church is a gift, and we must wisely and fearlessly deploy our human resources to the glory of God.

The wicked slave in the parable misuses his talent because of fear and laziness. You don't have to think too hard about the church today to recognize some of the same problems. There are often situations in which church leaders fail to act in a positive and bold way out of fear. This parable encourages us to question the wisdom of such inactivity and whether laziness might also be a factor. Sometimes, because of fear, we seek merely to hold on to what we have (the *status quo*) rather than work toward advancement. The master in this parable sees such fear as a mark of wickedness.

The fourth-century preacher John Chrysostom commented:

> Do you see how sins of omission are also met with extreme rejection? It is not only the covetous, the active doer of evil things and the adulterer, but also the one who fails to do good.[5]

The words of James 4:17 echo in our minds.

Gregory the Great from the sixth century reflected on the notion of hiding a talent in the earth and suggested that it represents "employing one's abilities in earthly affairs, failing to seek spiritual profit, never raising one's heart from earthly

thoughts."[6] We may be able to recognize these sorts of qualities in those churchgoers who remain on the sidelines of
commitment and whose behavior appears unaffected by the
gospel. They squander their talent.

Even the slave with the single talent was expected to put
that talent to good use. Just because a disciple might not have
the same abilities or resources as someone else does not
permit him or her to waste the gifts God has provided. The
second slave did not gain as much as the first, but he was not
for that reason given any less reward. He used what he had,
and received praise equal to that of the one who had used his
greater resources to gain greater profit.

***

If we can identify resources that God has given us, we
had better also be prepared to identify ways that we are
using them for his kingdom. When our master returns, he
will ask what we've been up to. We need a better answer
than maintaining the *status quo*.

Endnotes

[1] This chapter first appeared in *What Real Christianity
Looks Like: A Study of the Parables*, Berean Study Series, ed.
Ed. Gallagher (Florence, AL: Heritage Christian University
Press, 2016).

[2] W. D. Davies and D. C. Allison, *The Gospel according
to Saint Matthew*, 3 vols., International Critical Commentary (London: T&T Clark, 1988–97), 3.405.

[3] On money specifically, see Matthew 6:3–4; 19:21; on
wider use of resources, see 25:31–46.

[4] David L. Turner, *Matthew*, Baker Exegetical Commentary on the New Testament (Grand Rapids: Baker, 2008), 602.

[5] John Chrysostom, quoted in Manlio Simonetti, ed., *Matthew 14–28*, Ancient Christian Commentary on Scripture (Downers Grove, IL: IVP, 2002), 229.

[6] Gregory the Great, in Simonetti, *Matthew*, 223.

Chapter 9

Faith at the Cross

Approaching Luke 23:42

Uniquely among the Gospels, Luke records a conversation between Jesus at the cross on Golgotha and one of the criminals enduring crucifixion near him. Of the two criminals crucified on either side of Jesus (Mark 15:27; Luke 23:33), one parroted the words of the Jewish rulers and soldiers (Luke 23:35–38) by "hurling abuse at Him, saying, 'Are you not the Christ? Save Yourself and us!'" (23:39). The other criminal rebuked the first, asserting about Jesus, "this man has done nothing wrong" (23:41). He then turned toward Jesus and "was saying, 'Jesus, remember me when You come in Your kingdom!'" (23:42). The words with which Jesus responded give all penitent sinners hope in a glorious future with the Savior: "Truly I say to you, today you shall be with Me in Paradise" (23:43).

This "thief on the cross"—by the way, notice that Luke does not identify his crime, calling the two people crucified alongside Jesus "criminals"; the term "thief" comes from the KJV of the account in Matthew (27:38) and Mark (15:27). The Greek term used by Matthew and Mark (ληστης, *lēstēs*) suggests that the crime is not stealing but something more violent. Tracking this word through the Gospels would be an interesting study with some provocative implications for how these two people ended up being crucified by the Romans. But that is not our study at this moment. For now, we will use the term that Luke uses.

As I was saying, this "criminal on the cross" provides an amazing example of faith in an unlikely situation. Perhaps we in churches of Christ have sometimes overlooked his example because we have focused less on his words and more on the words of Jesus and their possible implications regarding the New Testament plan of salvation. Jesus clearly pronounces salvation upon this criminal. Other religious groups have, therefore, upheld this episode as a New Testament example of salvation through faith without baptism. However, since the conversation between Jesus and the criminal obviously occurred before "the death of the testator" (Heb 9:16), we do not have here an example of how to respond to God's "New Covenant" offer of salvation. The New Covenant was inaugurated with the death of Jesus; the criminal died under the Old Covenant.

Yet, just because the criminal lived and died under the Old Covenant does not mean that Christians today should not learn from and imitate his example of faith. Understanding the faith he expressed to Jesus on the cross requires that we give serious consideration to the meaning of his words, "when you come in your kingdom."

The Coming Kingdom

God's promise to David in 2 Samuel 7 constitutes one of the crucial themes in Israel's scripture. David had wanted to build a house for God, but Nathan the prophet declared to David that instead God would build a house for him (2 Sam 7:11). He meant that unlike Saul (7:15), David would establish a dynasty, and furthermore this dynasty would last forever. David's son would also be God's son (7:12–14). David and the Israelites probably considered this promise fulfilled with the coronation of David's son Solomon and the establishment of the Davidic line (cf. 1 Kgs 8:17–20, 25; 1 Chron 22:10), but some centuries later, during the reign of the Davidic king Ahaz (eighth century BC), Isaiah looked forward to the birth of a child who would sit "on the throne of David" (9:7 NASB). This one would be a "shoot from the stump of Jesse" (11:1). Contemporary with Isaiah, Micah envisioned a ruler coming from David's hometown of Bethlehem (5:2). Even while the Davidic dynasty still reigned, these prophets anticipated a future "Son of David" who would fulfill the hopes of Israel.

So it is with great excitement that we read in the very first verse of the New Testament (according to its present arrangement) that Jesus Christ (the Messiah) is the "Son of David," the One for whom Israel has been longing. The genealogy immediately following (Matt 1:2–17) establishes his Davidic credentials, and throughout the Gospel of Matthew Jesus is described as the "Son of David" (1:20; 9:27; 12:23; 15:22; 20:30–31; 21:9, 15; 22:41–46).

Confusion about the Kingdom

A reading of the Gospels demonstrates that the first-century Jews assumed that the "Son of David" would be essentially a reincarnation of David. Just as David won all his battles (1 Sam 17; 2 Sam 8), so also the Son of David would lead Israel to victory over her enemies. Peter no doubt had this in mind when he confessed that Jesus was the "Christ" (Messiah), the "anointed" king (Matt 16:16), as indicated by his readiness for battle when he thought the war was beginning (John 18:10). He did not understand that the kingdom of Jesus was not "of this world" and that the servants of Jesus should, therefore, not be fighting (John 18:36). Immediately following Peter's confession, Jesus began teaching what sort of Messiah he had come to be—one who would die on a cross and rise from the dead (Matt 16:21)—but, to put it kindly, this did not make sense to Peter (16:22–23).

The Son of David had come, but he was also David's Lord (Matt 22:41–46). The Son of David had come, but in his kingdom not the warriors but the peacemakers would be blessed (Matt 5:9). Needless to say, his contemporaries did not know what to make of him, and even his inner circle of disciples, after all his teaching on the kingdom, failed to understand his mission. At the very time it was coming to pass, "they all left Him and fled" (Mark 14:50), no doubt convinced that their hopes had been misplaced.

Even after the resurrection, the disciples still struggled to understand why the one they accepted as the Messiah had died. Luke records the account of the two disciples walking to Emmaus, discussing the final events of Jesus's life. When Jesus joined them, but before they could recognize him (24:15–16), they explained to him that "Jesus the Nazarene" had been "a prophet mighty in deed and word," but that "the chief priests and our rulers delivered Him to the sentence of death, and crucified Him" (24:19–20). The next verse reveals what this means for Jesus's messianic credentials. The two disciples say, "we were hoping that it was He who was going to redeem Israel" (24:21). The phrase "redeem

Israel" in the mouths of these disciples entails defeating
Israel's enemies (currently Rome) and re-establishing Israel
as a strong, independent nation in the likeness of David's
kingdom. These disciples "were hoping" that Jesus was the
"Son of David," the Messiah, who would in this way redeem
Israel. However, Jesus's death on a cross—something, they
thought, not supposed to happen to the Messiah (see again
Matt 16:21–23)—had apparently stifled these hopes. They
"were hoping" that Jesus was the Messiah up until the time
of his death; apparently that event caused them to stop
hoping for this. The fact that the body of Jesus has now been
reported missing (Luke 24:21–24) leads to increased confu-
sion on their part, not to fully revived hopes.

The Criminal's Confession

So, it is with some surprise that we read the criminal's statement to Jesus, "Remember me when you come in your kingdom." Finally, someone who gets it! This plea to Jesus
doubles as a confession of faith. The criminal on the cross,
just like Peter earlier, recognizes in Jesus the coming King,
the Messiah, who would rule God's kingdom. But, unlike
Peter and the rest of the disciples, the criminal somehow
understood that the cross did not signal the termination of
these hopes. Even while Jesus was hanging on a cross, about
to die a shameful death at the hands of his enemies, the criminal hanging next to him was still willing to acknowledge that
Jesus was a King, and not only that, but that after he died this
miserable death, he would yet come in his kingdom.

Who else at this moment of Jesus's agony would have
dared to make such a confession? Perhaps the women and
the Beloved Disciple who stood near Jesus's cross (John

19:25–26) retained some level of hope in who Jesus was. It seems more likely, however, given the level of understanding demonstrated by the other disciples, that even these who remained loyal to Jesus to the end did so not because they still considered him to be the coming King, but because they loved him and wanted to be with him in his hour of need. The Gospel accounts suggest that this one criminal alone, out of all of Jesus's disciples, maintained his faith that Jesus would still come in His kingdom.

Guessing at the Criminal's Background

One might ask how it is that the criminal came to have such great faith. Did something on Golgotha indicate to him that Jesus was in fact a King, and much more, that he would reign even after death? Did the sign above Jesus's head proclaiming him "King of the Jews" (Luke 23:38) convince the criminal of this? Surely the ridicule Jesus endured from the Jewish leadership (23:35–37) did not lead to the criminal's faith. Nor, indeed, did the behavior of Jesus's own disciples, most of whom abandoned their master at this time of trial. The criminal's faith, certainly his comprehension of the kingdom that far outstripped that of the disciples, cannot be explained if we surmise that Golgotha was the initial meeting place for Jesus and this criminal.

It seems altogether a better account of the facts to speculate that the criminal had been one of that nameless throng who had encountered Jesus during his earthly ministry. Perhaps he stood with other followers and heard the Sermon on the Mount, which so amazed "the crowds" (Matt 7:28). Perhaps he had been one of those five thousand men, or again one of the four thousand, who had received a full meal from Jesus's hand when moments earlier only a few fish and loaves were available (Matt 14:13–21; 15:32–38). More probably he was one of the "large crowds" (Matt 13:2) who listened while Jesus sat in a boat and taught about the nature of the kingdom of heaven. Certainly, his understanding of the kingdom evident in his statement to Jesus on the cross would be consistent with such a hypothesis. Perhaps he was even one of those many who were baptized in the name of Jesus during his ministry (John 4:1–2).

If the criminal did turn to the Lord at this time, he must have—like many others who encountered Jesus and even became his disciples (John 6:60!)—become frustrated with his new Rabbi and turned down a different path. He was charged and convicted of a crime. He was apprehended and brought to trial. The verdict was swift: crucifixion! Now, without hope, having betrayed his commitment to Jesus, he marched with his cross to a hill ominously named "The Skull." His cross was erected, and he was bound to it. He had only now to endure the pain and welcome death.

But, who should be placed on a cross right next to this condemned criminal, so close that he might look over and speak to him—none other than Jesus, the only one in this situation who could give him hope! Out of all the hills in Judea, the criminal and Jesus wound up on the very same one. Before there had been no hope for this criminal; now that he is next to Jesus, he again has hope, because he knows exactly who Jesus is—the King! And it is the King who can pardon offenses. The criminal now, after rebuking the other criminal and declaring that Jesus had done nothing wrong, can look at his Savior and say, "remember me when you come in Your kingdom." And he can receive the reply, "today you shall be with Me in paradise."

***

The story of the criminal on the cross provides a wonderful example of continued faith when no one else believes, and of God's care for the penitent sinner even at the last moment. May we remember that God likewise puts us next to a Savior in our moment of greatest need, and may we respond with the words of the criminal, "Remember me!"

Chapter 10

A Sickness Not Unto Death

Approaching John 11[1]

And our very Life came down here and bore our death
and killed it by the abundance of his life.

—Augustine, *Confessions* 4.12.19[2]

In the days of his flesh, Jesus offered up prayers and
supplications, with loud cries and tears, to the one who
was able to save him from death, and he was heard
because of his reverent submission (Heb 5:7).

Janet and Pat Moon are some of the best people I know,
some of the best Christian examples I've seen. They are
an example to me. I have accumulated a large debt to
them for their many kindnesses toward me, and I am grateful
to have this opportunity to dedicate a devotional essay to
them. I hope it provides encouragement to them and to all its
readers. And I look forward to many more years of working
alongside Janet and Pat. (In other words, don't retire!)

***

"This sickness is not unto death." We love that prognosis. The doctor invites us into his office for a consultation, so already we're a little nervous. He says, "We found something"—words that make our fists clench. We stop breathing, waiting for him to tell us when we're going to die. And then he says, "It's a sickness not unto death." Ah. Exhale. Loosen fists. We can relax a little. But, actually, of course, a doctor wouldn't say something like, "It's not a sickness unto death." He'd say something more like, "There's a ninety percent chance this is not a sickness unto death," or "chances are this is not a sickness unto death." Doctors don't like to speak in certainties; they like to hedge their bets.

But these are the words of Jesus in John 11:4, and Jesus does not hedge his bets. Jesus is always certain. So when he hears that Lazarus is sick, and responds by saying "this sickness is not unto death," we can be sure he knows of what he speaks. Do you know what happens next? Lazarus dies.

That's disappointing. Certainly Martha was disappointed in Jesus. "Lord, if you had been here, my brother would not have died" (v. 21). Certainly Martha's sister Mary was disappointed in Jesus: "Lord, if you had been here, my brother would not have died" (v. 32). They were the ones who had sent a note to Jesus telling him about Lazarus' illness (v. 3).

Jesus sometimes received messages like this. One time a centurion sent a message to Jesus telling him about his sick servant (Matt 8:5–13, Luke 7:1–10). The Jewish elders sent by this centurion testified about his good deeds, telling Jesus about how this Gentile had shown favor to God's people by building their synagogue. Then the centurion sent a second delegation to explain that he knew how authority works, so he was confident there would be no need for Jesus to come to his house; surely Jesus could get the job done from a distance (Luke 7:6–8). He was right. Jesus healed that servant without stepping foot in the centurion's house, without ever laying eyes on the centurion or the slave, perhaps without ever even knowing their names.

There was another time Jesus did something like that, when a Gentile woman from the region of Tyre and Sidon appealed to Jesus on behalf of her demon-possessed daughter (Matt 15:21–28, Mark 7:24–30). There was a bit of a back-and-forth between this mother and Jesus, but the result was the same as in the case of the centurion. Jesus simply pronounced the daughter cured without ever seeing her or touching her or saying any magic words. That's the kind of power Jesus has.

So, when Mary and Martha send a message to Jesus telling him that Lazarus is sick (John 11:3), surely in this instance, Jesus would act, and act quickly. After all, this is a family that Jesus knows well. He's been in their house before; he's friends with them, good friends. We actually read about Lazarus only here in the Gospel of John (in ch. 11, and in some later verses in the Gospel), but we read about the sisters Mary and Martha in one other passage, in the Gospel of Luke (10:38–42). That's the passage where Jesus is visiting in their home, and Martha is worried and bothered about so many things, but Mary has chosen the good part, because she's at the feet of Jesus listening to him. This is a family that Jesus knows so well that when Lazarus gets sick, Mary and Martha don't even mention his name; their message to Jesus simply says, "The one whom you love is sick" (John 11:3). They know full well that Jesus will know exactly who they're talking about, and they have every confidence that Jesus will drop everything for his dear friends and come immediately.

And so Jesus does ... nothing. He stays put. He waits. He does not respond to the urgent message of His friends. He does nothing at all.

Note the word "therefore" (or "accordingly" or "so," depending on your translation) in John 11:5–6. Because Jesus loved this family, He waited.

Lazarus Is Asleep

After a few days, Jesus tells His disciples that Lazarus has fallen asleep (v. 11). Of course, Jesus means he's died, but the disciples don't get it, and so He has to be more explicit with them: "Lazarus is dead" (v. 14). But at first He described Lazarus' death as sleep. That's reminiscent of the story about Jairus and his daughter (Matt 9:18–26, Mark 5:21–43, Luke 8:40–56). When Jesus arrived at Jairus' house and found all those people mourning the death of this young girl, Jesus told them, "She's not dead but asleep" (Mark 5:39). Of course, she was dead, she was not asleep. That's why the people who heard Jesus laughed at Him as a fool (Mark 5:40). They had checked her pulse: nothing. They had seen that she wasn't breathing. We can be confident that her heart had stopped beating and her brain activity had ceased. She was dead. So, why would Jesus say she was sleeping?

Sometimes in the morning I have to go to my kids' rooms and wake them up. I'll go into my sons' room, and hardly ever do I have to get my son Marvin up, but Josiah maybe. I'll say, "Josiah, get up. It's time to get ready for the day." Or in my daughters' room, it's not infrequent that I'll have to get Evelyn up. "Evelyn, get up and get dressed. Start doing your chore." I'll call out their names and tell them to get up. That's all it takes. Well, sort of. I'll have to do it a few times. But that's what Jesus means. She may have been dead to everyone else, but to Jesus she was just asleep, because all He had to do was to say, "Little girl, get up," and she got up (Mark 5:41–42).

The Bible often represents death as a type of sleep.[3] When the first martyr, Stephen, was being stoned to death in Acts 7, after he had prayed, the text says "he fell asleep" (v. 60). That's sort of a funny image, isn't it? He's being pelted with stones, and he falls asleep? Of course, what it means is that he died. The Bible I use regularly (the NRSV) thinks it sounds a little too funny, so they actually put in the text "he died," and then in the note they admit that literally the Greek says "he fell asleep." It's the same sort of thing when Paul says, "we shall not all sleep, but we shall all be changed" (1 Cor 15:51); he means that we won't all die, some of us will be alive when Jesus returns and the big transformation happens. Or there's that other passage, when Paul says that at the return of Jesus, those of us who are alive will not precede those who sleep (1 Thess 4:15). Again, he's talking about dead people. The Bible frequently uses the metaphor of sleep to refer to death. In the Old Testament there are all kinds of references to people who have died as "sleeping with their fathers" (e.g., 1 Kgs 11:43; 14:20; etc.). The Talmud describes sleep as a partial death: "Sleep is one-sixtieth of death."[4]

Why is that? What do sleep and death have in common? You can probably think of several similarities that I haven't thought about, but I think at least two similarities make a lot of sense. First of all, sleep is restful, and for that reason it is precious. We long for rest; we desire it. Sleep can be hard to come by. As I write this, my family has a new baby in the house, for the first time in about a decade. There's the saying, "sleep like a baby," and sometimes people turn that into a joke: "I sleep like a baby. I wake up every few hours screaming." Well, that is how a baby sleeps, but of course the saying refers to the fact that a baby can sleep through anything. In the middle of the day, with all kinds of noises around, a baby will sleep right through it all. I myself do not sleep like a baby in that sense. I've now started my fifth decade of life, and sleep is harder and harder to come by. Conditions have to be close to perfect for me to get a good sleep. I need white noise, but a particular type of white noise, created by a little fan. And I need complete darkness. And if anybody is moving in the room, I can't go to sleep. For me, sleep is precious because it's hard to come by. Especially now that we have a baby in the house again, sleep is harder to come by, and that makes it precious. We enjoy that rest when we get it. So also death. The Bible represents death as a type of sleep because death (for the righteous) is peaceful and restful. One ancient Jewish text says that those righteous who have died are in the hand of God (Wisdom of Solomon 3:1). The Gospel of Luke represents the righteous dead as in Abraham's bosom (Luke 16:22). Death is restful, like sleep.

Another way that death is like sleep is that it is temporary. It's not a permanent situation. We tend to think of it as permanent, but the one who has the power over life and death knows that it is very temporary.

That's what Jesus means that this sickness that Lazarus has contracted is not unto death. It will do no permanent damage. After all, this Jesus had earlier said in John's Gospel, "Truly I tell you, anyone who hears my word and believes him who sent me has eternal life, and does not come under judgment, but has passed from death to life" (5:24). And a little later, Jesus said, "Anyone who hears my words will never see death" (8:51).

In our eyes, Lazarus is dead. But Jesus knows he's just asleep, enjoying a temporary rest.

Jesus Let Him Die

Mary and Martha sent an urgent message to Jesus, and Jesus did nothing in response. He waited. He took his time. Mary and Martha were urgent, but Jesus wasn't.

It reminds me again of Jairus. Surely Jairus was very impatient with Jesus. I can imagine when that woman with the hemorrhage stopped Jesus, and Jesus took His time with her, Jairus must have been tapping his foot and looking at his watch and sighing audibly. Probably he said to Jesus, "Come on, we don't have time for this. My little girl needs us now!" I have no doubt that Jairus was feeling the pressure of time. Jesus was not. He was content to go slow. And He went so slow that while He was interacting with this hemorrhaging woman, the message came that Jairus needn't bother with the Teacher any longer, because the girl had died (Mark 5:35). She died because Jesus was so slow. Jesus let her die.

God sometimes lets people die.

Recently I went to the hospital with some other people from church to deliver gift bags to patients and family members in waiting rooms. I went into some hospital rooms and talked to the people laid up in bed. One lady, maybe my age or a little younger, was happy for a visitor. She had been in that hospital bed for a week with an infection. She showed me how swollen she was. Before that she had been in another hospital in a different city to run some tests and do some procedures for which our local hospital wasn't equipped. So she'd been away from home for a while. Her husband was keeping their autistic son, and of course Mama does most of the work at home, so the husband was struggling. He didn't know how to help his kid through homework, so while the mama was in the hospital out-of-state, they would videochat so she could help the son with homework. I asked her how long she would be in the hospital. She didn't know; she had heard no sort of timetable. I asked if I could pray for her. She welcomed it. So I prayed that God would bless her and her family, that He would be good to them in this situation, and I prayed that God would heal her. I don't know what God will do. I know that James says we should pray without doubting (1:6), and I don't doubt that God will do the best thing in the situation, but I doubt that I know what the best thing is. I do know this: sometimes God lets people die.

I went into another room, and found an older couple, maybe in their seventies. The man was in the bed, unconscious. The wife was on the couch catching a nap, but she was happy when someone from a church walked in. She told me about her husband, about his heart condition. And she asked me to pray for them. Again, I prayed for comfort and for healing. But I couldn't offer any assurances of recovery. I couldn't tell this woman that her husband's sickness was not unto death. I wasn't sure what God would do.

We have been trained to think that the clock is everything. We have seen enough doctors shows on television to know how this works, or we've experienced it in hospitals for ourselves. There's only limited time to save a life. I grew up with the show *ER*, and I saw scene after scene of someone bleeding out or unconscious or suffering in some other way, being wheeled into the ER on a gurney. And sometimes the doctor would climb up onto the gurney and straddle the patient and beat on the person's chest. People were running around and everybody was yelling "STAT!" We know that if a person's life is going to be saved, time is of the essence. We've seen the monitors with those spiky lines and the constant beep, beep, beep. And we know that if ever that line goes flat, and that beep stops beeping, becoming merely one long note, everything's over. That's it. The person has died, and that's all there is to it. There's no coming back from the dead. It's permanent. We've even seen (how many times?) on TV when the doctor has promised that he's not going to let this patient die, so the doctor is doing chest compressions or some other procedure, furiously attempting to ensure survival over which he has no control, and when the monitor displays that flatline and the beep becomes one solid note, the doctor keeps working on the patient until finally his colleagues convince him that there's no use. When you're talking life and death, time matters. You've got to be urgent.

But in John 11, when Jesus hears about Lazarus, He displays no urgency at all. Martha and Mary are urgent, but not Jesus. Same for the Jairus story. Jesus takes His time. He doesn't realize that time is so all-important when it comes to saving lives. Because, as it turns out, time doesn't matter to Jesus at all.

Death is no impediment to the saving call of Jesus.

It doesn't matter if Jairus' daughter's heart has stopped beating. Jesus just needs to wake her up. It doesn't matter if Lazarus has been dead so long he stinketh. Jesus just needs to call, "Lazarus, come forth!"

God sometimes lets people die because death does not stand in the way of God.

Abundant Life

Just like Martha (John 11:21) and Mary (v. 32), there were some other people there in Bethany mourning the death of Lazarus, who also thought that Jesus could have prevented that death if only He had been there (v. 37). This is a faithful response, but it also displays imperfect faith, because it does not acknowledge that Jesus controls life and death. He created life (John 1:1–4), and there is no time limit on Jesus's ability to confer life. After all, "just as the Father has life in himself, so he has granted the Son to have life in himself" (5:26). Jesus told Martha, "I am the resurrection and the life" (11:25).

In John 10:10, Jesus says that He has come to distribute life to people, and He specifies: "a life more abundant." We have been misled by our American culture into thinking that what Jesus came to deliver to us is equivalent to the American Dream. (Some preachers on TV have contributed to this error.) We often think that the abundant life Jesus wants for us is basically Life, Liberty, and the Pursuit of Happiness. He wants us healthy, wealthy, and wise. The New Living Translation actually renders John 10:10, "a rich and satisfying life."

This is all wrong. Remember that Jesus is the one who has life in Himself, so that He can distribute life to whomever He will. Right before Jesus says that the Father has granted Him to have life in Himself, He says, "the dead will hear the voice of the Son of God, and those who hear will live" (5:25). A couple chapters after the Good Shepherd Discourse, Jesus will remind His audience that only if a seed "dies" in the ground will it become a life-giving plant (John 12:24). This is abundant life—life so abundant that not even death can overcome it. Jesus has come to so fill us with life that it carries over even into death—nay, rather, it continually increases even in death. "Man is called to a fullness of life which far exceeds the dimensions of his earthly existence, because it consists in sharing the very life of God."[5]

Death is simply sleep. It is temporary and restful. As the poet says, "One short sleep past, we wake eternally and death shall be no more." That doesn't dull the pain that we feel when loved ones die. Well, it should dull the pain a little. And Jesus knows about the pain that death brings. "You will be sorrowful, but your sorrow will be turned into joy" (John 16:20).

Death is all around us. It seems like we hear about some new cause of cancer every other day, or some new shooting, or some natural disaster. Life itself is going to kill us. And we can't control it.

The assurance Jesus gave in the case of Lazarus, He gives to us all. It doesn't matter what the doctor says. That prognosis is irrelevant. Jesus gives us our prognosis.

This sickness is not unto death.

***

"Son of Adam," said Aslan, "go into that thicket and pluck the thorn that you will find there, and bring it to me."

Eustace obeyed. The thorn was a foot long and sharp as a rapier.

"Drive it into my paw, Son of Adam," said Aslan, holding up his right fore-paw and spreading out the great pad toward Eustace.

"Must I?" said Eustace.

"Yes," said Aslan.

Then Eustace set his teeth and drove the thorn into the Lion's pad. And there came out a great drop of blood, redder than all redness that you have ever seen or imagined. And it splashed into the stream over the dead body of the King. At the same moment the doleful music stopped. And the dead King began to be changed. His white beard turned to gray, and from gray to yellow, and got shorter and vanished altogether; and his sunken cheeks grew round and fresh, and the wrinkles were smoothed, and his eyes opened, and his eyes and lips both laughed, and suddenly he leaped up and stood before them—a very young man, or a boy.[6]

Endnotes

[1] This chapter first appeared in *Serving the Lord: A Festschrift for Freddie Patrick Moon and Janet Stewart Moon*, Heritage Legacy Series (Florence, AL: Heritage Chrisitan University Press, 2022).

[2] Augustine, *Confessions*, trans. Thomas Williams (Indianapolis: Hackett, 2019), 53.

[3] For references in the Old Testament and for discussion, see Jon D. Levenson, *Resurrection and the Restoration of Israel: The Ultimate Victory of the God of Life* (New Haven, CT: Yale University Press, 2006), 186–87. Outside Jewish tradition, the hero Gilgamesh also compares existence in the Netherworld to sleep (tablet 9); see the translation of Andrew George, *The Epic of Gilgamesh*, 2d ed. (London: Penguin, 2020), 69. Levenson takes this relationship between sleep and death more negatively than I do. He understands sleep's similarity to death to mean that sleep itself was considered dangerous, and waking to be a type of miraculous resurrection in which God restores one's soul.

Perhaps he is correct that early on the relationship was conceived in this way, that both sleep and death are dangerous, but I suggest that as believers continued to reflect on the relationship, they came to see that the opposite understanding could also be true, *viz.*, that neither sleep nor death were dangerous or permanent.

[4] Babylonian Talmud, tractate *Berakhot* 57b (at §13 in the presentation of the Talmud at sefaria.org), quoted (but mis-cited) in Levenson , *Resurrection*, 74, 186.

[5] John Paul II, *Evangelium Vitae* (1995), §2.

[6] C. S. Lewis, *The Silver Chair*, The Chronicles of Narnia (New York: HarperCollins, 1953), ch. 16, p. 252.

Chapter 11

Not Under the Law
Approaching Galatians 5:18[1]

In Genesis, God commanded Abraham to ensure that "Every male among you shall be circumcised" (Gen 17:10). This "sign of the covenant between me and you" (17:11) should be kept "throughout your generations" (17:12), and it applied to even those not born into the family but acquired in some other way (17:12–13). The commandments delivered to the people by Moses also stipulated that every eight-day old baby Israelite boy should be circumcised (Lev 12:3), and any uncircumcised person could not celebrate the Passover (Exod 12:44, 48). While the Old Testament does not mention circumcision much beyond these references (a key exception is Josh 5), it is clear that the males of the family of Abraham had to be circumcised or risk being cut off from the people (Gen 17:14).

According to the apostle Paul, there are children of Abraham (Gal 3:29) who do not need to be circumcised (5:2) —or, rather, who will find themselves cut off from the family of Abraham if they are circumcised (5:4). These people do not need circumcision because they belong to Christ (3:29).

In fact, "in Christ Jesus neither circumcision nor uncircumcision counts for anything" (5:6; cf. 6:15; 1 Cor 7:19; Rom 2:25–29).

This insistence on Paul's part makes it sound like he believes his readers are not obligated to keep the Torah. Indeed, Paul asserts that "if you are led by the Spirit, you are not subject to the law" (5:18). This statement comes after a couple verses contrasting the Spirit and the flesh (5:16–17), and the epistle before this point has already taught readers to associate the law with the flesh (cf. 3:3; 4:23, 29). Christians should be led by the Spirit because they are children of God, and "God has sent the Spirit of his Son into our hearts, crying, 'Abba! Father!'" (4:6).

And yet, Paul can also say in this same letter that those who are circumcised do not keep the law (6:13), but that the law is fulfilled in a single command, "You shall love your neighbor as yourself" (5:14; cf. Lev 19:18)—certainly a command that Paul expects the Galatians to feel bound to obey. While these Galatian Christians are not under the law, they do fulfill the law.

Freed from the Torah

What is this law that Paul keeps talking about? The Greek word is *nomos* (νόμος), which is the word used in the Septuagint—the Greek translation of the Old Testament—for the Hebrew word *torah*. This Hebrew word is now (and for many centuries) used as the title for the first five books of the Bible, the Torah of Moses or Pentateuch. But *torah* could also refer to Scripture as a whole, the entire Old Testament; such a usage of *torah* or *nomos* appears both in the New Testament (John 10:34; 15:25; Gal 3:10; 1 Cor 14:21) and in rabbinic literature.[2] Then again, the word *torah* could refer specifically to the law code in the Pentateuch (see, e.g., Rom 2:13; Gal 6:13). As Stephen Westerholm asserts, "Paul sometimes uses 'law' (νόμος) to mean the Old Testament Scriptures, or more specifically the Pentateuch. But according to his most frequent usage, 'law' refers to the Sinaitic legislation."[3]

The word *nomos* appears 194 times in the New Testament, and 32 times in Galatians, second only to Romans (74x). The first appearance of *nomos* in Galatians provides a helpful entrypoint.

> ...yet we know that a person is justified not by the works of the law but through faith in Jesus Christ. And we have come to believe in Christ Jesus, so that we might be justified by faith in Christ, and not by doing the works of the law, because no one will be justified by the works of the law (Gal 2:16).

Paul's burden in this letter is to disassociate justification from works of law. While it is difficult to know much about Paul's opponents in this letter, they seem to be (probably Jewish-)Christian missionaries who encouraged the Galatians to be circumcised and to observe other commands in the Jewish Torah, probably with the view that Torah observance marked one out as belonging to God.[4] Given this background, we can relate "law" here specifically to Torah (an equation we can probably make throughout the letter). Paul attempted to disassociate justification from works of Torah, "for if justification comes through the Torah, then Christ died for nothing" (2:21); and "no one is justified before God by the Torah" (3:11); and "You who want to be justified by the Torah have cut yourselves off from Christ" (5:4).

Paul sometimes says in this letter some rather negative things about the Torah, things that were no doubt shocking to some of his contemporaries. The Torah was added because of transgressions (3:19), not only to highlight the problem of sin but apparently even to intensify the problem. The authority of the Torah was temporary, merely a tutor to lead us to Christ (3:24–25). The Torah in a sense imprisoned us (3:23), but now we are freed through Christ. Indeed, the Torah is a kind of enslaver (4:1, 21–31; 5:1).

It is no wonder that Paul considers it good news to inform Christians that they are not "under the Torah," a phrase he uses eleven times in his letters. While Jews are under the Torah (1 Cor 9:20; cf. Gal 3:23; 4:4–5), those who believe in Christ are not (Rom 6:14–15; Gal 5:18), just as Paul does not consider himself to be (1 Cor 9:20). Paul wrote his letter to the Galatian Christians in order to explain this fact to some who wanted to be under the Torah (Gal 4:21).

Not being "under the Torah" means that Christians are not obligated to keep the commands of the Sinaitic law code. (Even those "under the Torah" do not do the Torah, as both Paul [Rom 3:10–20] and Jesus [John 7:19] assert.) Sometimes Paul mentions specific commands that Christians do not need to observe, such as the circumcision command—as we have seen—but also food laws (Rom 14:14) and holy days (Rom 14:5–6). But Paul surely has more in view than just these ritual commands (or boundary markers, marking off Jews from Gentiles) when he says (5:18) that Christians are not "under the Torah." Paul, in fact, never says that Christians "do" or "perform" the laws of the Torah,[5] and Paul does not direct his Christian readers to the Torah in the context of laying down Christian ethical demands, such as avoiding idolatry and sexual immorality (e.g., 1 Cor 6:12–20; 10:14–22; 1 Thess 4:3–8)—or, at least, not the Pentateuchal commands that explicitly address these sins. The only exception is Paul's quoting the Fourth Commandment, "honor your father and mother" (Eph 6:1–3; cf. 1 Cor 9:9; 14:34; 1 Tim 5:18). The Torah is holy (Rom 7:12) and provides a guide for Christian ethics (cf. 1 Cor 5:1–13; 10:1–14; Rom 15:4; 2 Tim 3:16–17) but is not binding on Christians.

This was the point driven home by Alexander Campbell in 1816 in his famous "Sermon on the Law," a sermon that, he says, essentially drove him toward the path of what became the American Restoration Movement.[6] He insisted on jettisoning as unscriptural the old distinction between moral laws and civil laws and ceremonial laws in the Torah, with the idea that Christians were still obliged to keep the moral laws.[7] In churches of Christ, the insistence that we look to the New Testament for instructions binding on Christians rather than to the Old Testament has been an essential element of "rightly dividing the word of truth" (2 Tim 2:15).[8]

And yet, Campbell—who delivered a series of chapel speeches on the Pentateuch that were later published[9]—would not agree with the statement sometimes made about churches of Christ (not only by those outside our churches!) that we do not consider the Old Testament authoritative. I wish to make a distinction between authority, on the one hand, and binding, on the other. In saying that the Mosaic legislation is not binding on Christians, I also want to uphold the truth of 2 Timothy 3:16–17, which I think we can do by keeping before us these commonly agreed principles: (1) we are not saved by adherence to the laws of the Torah; (2) from the laws of the Torah can be derived principles that can guide our ethical practice (e.g., care for the poor) in harmony with principles broadly attested in Scripture (e.g., mercy, compassion, justice); (3) the laws of the Torah reveal to us something about the character of our God, including his justice, holiness, and mercy.[10]

Fulfilling the Torah

According to Paul, Christians are not "under the Torah" but they do "fulfill the Torah." The apostle makes such a claim in three passages.

> the just requirement of the Torah might be fulfilled in us, who walk not according to the flesh but according to the Spirit (Rom 8:4).

> Owe no one anything, except to love one another; for the one who loves another has fulfilled the Torah. The commandments, "You shall not commit adultery; You shall not murder; You shall not steal; You shall not covet"; and any other commandment, are summed up in this word, "Love your neighbor as yourself." Love does no wrong to a neighbor; therefore, love is the fulfilling of the Torah (Rom 13:8–10).

> For the whole Torah is fulfilled in a single commandment, "You shall love your neighbor as yourself" (Gal 5:14).

We've seen that Christians do not "do" the commandments of the Torah, but Paul says that those led by the Spirit "fulfill" the Torah, specifically by concentrating on a single one of its commandments, the very one Jesus highlighted as the second greatest commandment (Matt 22:34–40), the one found in Leviticus 19:18 and enjoining love of neighbor. Whereas the Torah itself threatened punishment on the disobedient but even so was not able to penetrate the stony hearts of those who fell under its obligations, those led by the Spirit serve God not out of fear but out of love through the Spirit of Christ who now dwells within them. We do not concentrate on the flesh and its works (things regulated by the commands of the Torah) but being led by the Spirit we participate with the Spirit in producing the fruit—note how each one of the fruit in Galatians 5:22–23 are aspects of Leviticus 19:18—that allows us to fulfill the righteous requirement of the Torah.

***

Christians are no longer under the law but are instead "under grace" (Rom 6:14)—which might sound as if the gospel includes no ethical demands. Paul immediately rejects such an inference with a characteristic, "God forbid!" (6:15). The same ideas play out in Romans 8, but now with the language of the Spirit guiding Christians. This is the language Paul uses in Galatians 5, as he contrasts the life in the Spirit from the life under the law. Being freed from the law's demands is liberating for the believer precisely because the Spirit's guidance allows us to fulfill the requirements of the law out of love for our saving God.

Endnotes

[1] This chapter first appeared in *Led by God's Spirit: A Practical Study of Galatians* 5:22–26, Berean Study Series, ed. Bill Bagents (Florence, AL: Heritage Christian University Press, 2023).

[2] Solomon Schechter, *Aspects of Rabbinic Theology: Major Concepts of the Talmud* (New York: Macmillan, 1909), 116–26.

[3] Stephen Westerholm, *Perspectives Old and New on Paul: The "Lutheran" Paul and His Critics* (Grand Rapids: Eerdmans, 2004), 297, and see the fuller argument on pp. 298–300. Westerholm further argues (pp. 335–40) that Paul's use of the Greek word *nomos* corresponds to the use of the Hebrew term *torah* among Hebrew-speakers. The word *nomos* could also be used in a more general way (cf. Rom 7:21); see the first definition in Frederick William Danker, ed., *A Greek-English Lexicon of the New Testament and Other Early Christian Literature*, 3d ed. (Chicago: University of Chicago Press, 2000), 677–78.

[4] John M. G. Barclay, "Mirror-Reading a Polemical Letter: Galatians as a Test Case," *Journal for the Study of the New Testament* 31 (1987): 73–93.

[5] See Westerholm, *Perspectives Old and New*, 433–37. This statement, as Westerholm says, assumes that Paul does not have Christians in mind in Romans 2:14–15.

[6] Alexander Campbell, "Sermon on the Law," *Millennial Harbinger* (September 1846), 493–521.

[7] Westerholm, *Perspectives Old and New*, 437, agrees with Campbell, though he also points out that Paul hints at something like a distinction between moral and ceremonial laws in Romans 2:25–29.

[8] See, for instance, the sermons under this title by N. B. Hardeman, *Hardeman's Tabernacle Sermons*, vol. 1 (1922; repr. Henderson, TN: Freed-Hardeman University, 1990).

[9] Alexander Campbell, *Familiar Lectures on the Pentateuch* (Cincinnati: Bosworth, 1867).

[10] For more on the role that the laws of the Torah can play in Christianity, see Ed Gallagher, *The Book of Exodus: Explorations in Christian Theology,* Cypress Bible Study Series (Florence, AL: Heritage Christian University Press, 2020), 161–94; Ed Gallagher, *The Sermon on the Mount: Explorations in Christian Practice,* Cypress Bible Study Series (Florence, AL: Heritage Christian University Press, 2021), 51–63.

Chapter 12

The Bible on Slavery

Approaching Ephesians 6:4–9[1]

arriet Jacobs tells the story about how the slave masters initiated a worship service for slaves. The very first time she attended such a worship service, the sermon's text was Ephesians 6:5.

Of course it was.

After summarizing the homily, Jacobs describes the reaction from her fellow slaves: "We went home, highly amused at brother Pike's gospel teaching, and we determined to hear him again. I went the next Sabbath evening, and heard pretty much a repetition of the last discourse."[2] I'm confident that no one will be surprised to learn that Ephesians 6:5 was a popular text for sermons directed at slaves in the nineteenth-century southern United States.[3]

The Bible and slavery—this is a difficult discussion, for several reasons. The legacy of American slavery is still so very painful, and the use of the Bible to undergird the institution of slavery is high on the list of embarrassments for Christians (near the Crusades). But it's not like the Bible says nothing useful for opponents of slavery; two centuries ago,

Christian Scripture played a crucial role in the abolitionist movement.[4] Lincoln had reason to say that both sides in the American Civil War, North and South, "read the same Bible, and pray to the same God; and each invokes His aid against the other." More than that, both cited the Bible against the other side.[5] A discussion about the Bible and slavery is difficult most of all because the Bible simply does not say what we wish it said about slavery.[6] We wish the Bible said that slavery is wrong, sinful, an affront against God and against human beings made in the image of God. Instead, the Bible says, "Slaves, obey your masters" (Eph 6:5).

There's more in the Bible—and in Paul!—relevant to this issue than just Ephesians 6. As Esau McCaulley points out: "Whatever we might say of the Pauline slave texts, few would argue that Paul's thoughts on slavery stand at the center of his theological world."[7] If we're really going to understand what the Bible says about slavery, we've got to put these instructions to slaves and masters into a broader biblical context, and it would be helpful if we knew something about slavery in the ancient world and how ancient people thought about slavery. The whole discussion continues to be distressingly relevant in the twenty-first century. We've already mentioned the lingering effects of American slavery that was abolished more than a century and a half ago. Though slavery is no longer legal, human trafficking is a present concern, and by some estimates there are more slaves in the world today than there ever have been before.[8]

Slavery in the World of the Bible

The Roman Empire into which Christianity was born constituted one of the major slave societies in the history of the world.[9] Scholars often talk about specifically five major slave societies: ancient Athens, ancient Rome, and—in the eighteenth and nineteenth centuries—the southern United States, the Caribbean islands, and Brazil. These were societies that did not just have slaves but in which the importance of slavery within the society reached a certain threshold (as defined by modern scholars) so that they can be classified as "slave societies." Usually the criteria for defining a "slave society" include a high percentage of enslaved people (about 20% or more of the population) and slavery's importance to the working of the economy. The Roman Empire, and in particular Italy and especially the city of Rome (where Paul may have been when he wrote Ephesians), qualify as a slave society based on these factors. But though ancient Rome and the southern United States in the nineteenth century were both slave societies, the two societies practiced slavery in different ways, particularly in regard to the relationship between slavery and race: while American slavery came to be associated closely with African descent, Ancient Romans did not derive their slaves from any particular ethnic group or nationality.[10] As Noel Lenski has stressed,

> This absence of racial criteria in Roman slavery cannot be emphasized strongly enough as a crucial element differentiating the ideology, economics, ethics, and praxis of slavery in Rome versus the modern world.[11]

Strange to say, there was no abolitionist movement in the ancient world. There were no Frederick Douglasses wandering the Roman Empire preaching about the evils of the institution of slavery and calling for its elimination. Though slavery has existed in many societies on earth throughout history, a movement for the abolition of slavery arose only in relatively modern times (especially in the eighteenth and nineteenth centuries in the Western world). Unfortunately, when Christianity became the official religion of the Roman Empire in the fourth century, the slave system continued.[12]

While the Bible does contain commandments regulating (rather than abolishing) slavery (cf. Exod 21:1–6; Lev 25:39–55; Deut 15:12–18), and while American slaveholders did quote the Bible in their favor, the Bible contains enough material that sits uneasily with the practice of slavery that masters were not comfortable allowing their slaves full access to Scripture. The historian Thomas Kidd explains:

> White critics had worried that Christianizing African Americans, especially slaves, was dangerous. Doing so might give slaves notions about their rights as Christians and about God's deliverance for those in bondage.[13]

They were right to worry. After all, one of the major stories in the Bible—the most important story in the Old Testament—centers on Israelite slaves rebelling from their Egyptian masters. Prominent abolitionists, including some who had themselves been enslaved, took inspiration from Scripture: both Nat Turner and Frederick Douglass were preachers, and Harriet Tubman's nickname was Moses. While the Bible might not straightforwardly say that holding people in slavery is sinful, Paul does condemn "menstealers" (1 Tim 1:10; cf. Exod 21:16; Deut 24:7),[14] and there are plenty of commandments about loving neighbors and avoiding anger and treating others better than yourself, which would make the practice of slaveholding fairly obviously inconsistent with Scripture. For these very reasons, an edition of the Bible was produced specifically for slaves, which omitted all the parts that might make the slaves think that God was not necessarily on the side of the master.[15]

In the early days of the USA, southern slaveholders realized (as did northerners and foreigners) that the rhetoric of liberty and equality sat uncomfortably with the flourishing of slavery in the South. In 1788, during the process of the ratification of the US Constitution, Charles Cotesworth Pinckney of South Carolina argued in favor of the proposed Constitution based in part on the fact that it lacked a Bill of Rights (which, of course, came later as the first ten amendments).

> "Such bills," he asserted, "generally begin with declaring that all men are by nature born free. Now, we should make that declaration with a very bad grace, when a large part of our property consists in men who are actually born slaves."[16]

A generation later, another South Carolinian, William Harper, insisted that the Revolutionary generation was actually exaggerating when it declared the equality of all men.

> Whatever may have been said in the fervor of their zeal by those who were in pursuit of the greatest practicable

liberty, such natural equality and universal freedom never did and never can exist.[17]

To the extent that notions of liberty and equality are seen as connected to the religion of the Bible, to such an extent Christianity is inconsistent with holding slaves.[18]

In the ancient world, not everyone was convinced in the equality of all people. No less an authority than Aristotle argued that some people were born to be slaves.[19] But there were people such as the Stoic philosophers Seneca (*Epistle* 47, first century AD) and Epictetus (*Discourses* 1.13, early second century AD) who argued not only for the humane treatment of slaves but for the basic recognition that slaves and masters were essentially equal in their humanity, that slavery was not a natural condition. Still, Seneca did not argue for, or even contemplate, the abolition of slavery—nor did Epictetus, though he was himself a freed slave.

While slaves appear not infrequently in the New Testament, in the parables of Jesus,[20] for instance, there is not much instruction about how slaves should behave or how masters should treat slaves (the latter, only Eph 6:9; Col 4:1).[21] Paul does not campaign for abolition, but he does tell slaves to obtain their freedom if the opportunity should arise (1 Cor 7:21), and he uses all his moral and apostolic authority to persuade Philemon to manumit Onesimus.[22] (Manumission was, in fact, surprisingly common for Roman slaves.)[23] But mostly Paul wants slaves to focus on representing Christ in the world and not on obtaining freedom.

> Were you a bondservant when called? Do not be concerned about it. (But if you can gain your freedom, avail yourself of the opportunity.) For he who was called

in the Lord as a bondservant is a freedman of the Lord. Likewise he who was free when called is a bondservant of Christ. (1 Cor 7:21–22)[24]

If it be asked whether Paul would have agreed more with Aristotle or with Seneca and Epictetus concerning the basic equality of slaves and masters, there can really be no doubt of the answer, not for the apostle who wrote the following.

> There is no longer Jew or Greek, there is no longer slave or free, there is no longer male and female; for all of you are one in Christ Jesus (Gal 3:28).

> For in the one Spirit we were all baptized into one body— Jews or Greeks, slaves or free—and we were all made to drink of one Spirit (1 Cor 12:13).

> In that renewal there is no longer Greek and Jew, circumcised and uncircumcised, barbarian, Scythian, slave and free; but Christ is all and in all! (Col 3:11)[25]

Maybe the Bible isn't as straightforward and explicit on the issue of slavery as we would like (nor was anyone else until just a few centuries ago), but it was straightforward enough on universal human equality and value to be a dangerous book in the hands of a slave, as the slaveholders of the American South realized all too clearly.[26] And if we view the issue from a wider lens—does the Bible encourage or discourage oppressing others? does the Bible generally side with the oppressor or the oppressed?—the matter becomes even clearer.[27]

The Life of Faith and Slavery in the Bible

But the truth about the Bible on slavery is not that the Bible calls for the elimination of slavery but that the Bible calls on all of us who would be children of God and imitators of Christ to think of ourselves as slaves of God and of one another.

It was our Lord who said:

Whoever wishes to be first among you must be slave of all (Mark 10:44).

It was our Lord who, "knowing that the Father had given all things into his hands, and that he had come from God and was going to God, got up from the table, took off his outer robe, and tied a towel around himself" (John 13:3–4) to wash the apostles' feet, after which he instructed, "I have set you an example, that you should do as I have done to you" (13:15).

It was our Lord "who, though he was in the form of God, did not regard equality with God as something to be exploited, but emptied himself, taking the form of a slave" (Phil 2:6–7).

In the instructions to slaves and masters in Ephesians 6, Paul charged slaves to obey their masters as if they were obeying Christ, to give service with enthusiasm, because they are "slaves of Christ" (6:5–8). And then Paul turned to the masters and commanded, "masters, do the same to them. Stop threatening them, for you know that both of you have the same Master in heaven, and with him there is no partiality" (6:9). What are the implications of those six words, "masters, do the same to them"? Immediately after telling slaves to serve their masters as if they were serving Christ, he bids the masters to "do the same" to their slaves. Can he really be telling masters to serve their slaves as if they were serving Christ? Such are the implications of the gospel, because in Christ there is no slave or free—we are all one (Gal 3:28), and we are all slaves. This is the radical, upside down world of Christianity, in which those who mourn are considered fortunate (Matt 5:4) and those who are persecuted should rejoice (5:10–12) and people turn the other cheek (5:39) and love their enemies (5:44) and take up their cross (16:24). In a religion in which the wisdom of God is revealed primarily in "Christ crucified, a stumbling block to Jews and foolishness to Gentiles" (1 Cor 1:23), yes, the apostle can tell slaveholders to serve their slaves as if serving Christ. In fact, he can tell us all to "be subject to one another out of reverence for Christ" (Eph 5:21). As Alexander Campbell wrote of the treatment of masters toward slaves at the very time that slavery was still practised in his home state of Virginia: "He is just to do for him as his slave what he would have his slave do for him, were he himself to become the slave and his servant the master."[28]

***

The Bible does not say what we wish it said about slavery. What the Bible says is that we are all slaves (Luke 17:10!), that we should serve one another. Idealistic? Perhaps. But Jesus has shown us the way. We can feel satisfied about our own practice of Christianity when we are fully conformed to the image of our Lord who became a slave for us.

Endnotes

[1] This chapter first appeared in *For the Glory of God: Christ and the Church in Ephesians*, Berean Study Series, ed. Ed Gallagher (Florence, AL: Heritage Christian University Press, 2021).

[2] Harriet Jacobs, *Incidents in the Life of a Slave Girl* (Boston, 1861); ed. Frances Smith Foster and Richard Yarborough, Norton Critical Edition, 2d ed. (New York: Norton, 2019), 62, in ch. 13, "The Church and Slavery."

[3] Thomas S. Kidd, *America's Religious History: Faith, Politics, and the Shaping of a Nation* (Grand Rapids: Zondervan, 2019), 114. Howard Thurman reported that his formerly enslaved grandmother told him that Ephesians 6:5 formed the basis of a white minister's sermon to the slaves at least three or four times per year; Howard Thurman, *Jesus and the Disinherited* (Boston: Beacon, 1976), 30.

[4] As an example: George Bourne, *The Book and Slavery Irreconcilable* (Philadelphia: Sanderson, 1816).

[5] For a tame example, see the collection of friendly letters from Francis Wayland (anti-slavery) and Richard Fuller (pro-slavery), both Baptist ministers, originally written in 1847, and recently re-edited in *Domestic Slavery Considered as a Scriptural Institution*, ed. Nathan A. Finn and Keith Harper (Macon, GA: Mercer University Press, 2008).

[6] See the similar formulation in Esau McCaulley, *Reading While Black: African American Biblical Interpretation as an Exercise in Hope* (Downers Grove, IL: IVP, 2020), 139, 151.

[7] McCaulley, *Reading While Black*, 18.

[8] Wikipedia, "Slavery"; or, for a more authoritative source, Annie Bunting and Joel Quirk, eds., *Contemporary*

Slavery: Popular Rhetoric and Political Practice (Vancouver: UBC Press, 2017).

[9] For recent discussion of the concept of a slave society, see Noel Lenski and Catherine M. Cameron, eds., *What Is a Slave Society? The Practice of Slavery in Global Perspective* (Cambridge: Cambridge University Press, 2018).

[10] On Roman slavery, start with Keith Bradley, *Slavery and Society at Rome* (Cambridge: Cambridge University Press, 1994), who does note (p. 66 n. 10) that some Romans (e.g., Cicero, *On the Consular Provinces* 10; Livy, 35.49.8; 36.17.5) considered certain races (Asiatic Greeks, Syrians, Jews) to be born for slavery. See also Peter Garnsey, *Ideas of Slavery from Aristotle to Augustine* (Cambridge: Cambridge University Press, 1996), 170–71, on Aristotle and Philo. Peter Hunt notes: "though not racist in the modern sense, ancient slavery was often justified by a sense of ethnic superiority"; Peter Hunt, *Ancient Greek and Roman Slavery* (Malden, MA: Wiley-Blackwell, 2018), 29.

[11] Noel Lenski, "Ancient Slaveries and Modern Ideology," in Lenski and Cameron, *What Is a Slave Society*, 106–47, at 139. See also Lenski's wider discussion (pp. 134–45) on the differences between slavery in Rome and in the US South. Jemar Tisby considers this argument from different practices of enslavement (in his discussion, between the Ancient Near East and the American South) to be the strongest antislavery argument for the nineteenth-century abolitionists; *The Color of Compromise: The Truth about the American Church's Complicity in Racism* (Grand Rapids: Zondervan, 2019), 84–85.

[12] Mary E. Sommar, *The Slaves of the Churches: A History* (Oxford: Oxford University Press, 2020). Did master/slave

relations improve? See Garnsey, *Ideas of Slavery*, 210n4. Some Christians, such as Gregory of Nyssa in the fourth century, considered it sinful to hold people in slavery; see the analysis of Ilaria Ramelli, *Social Justice and the Legitimacy of Slavery: The Role of Philosophical Asceticism from Ancient Judaism to Late Antiquity* (Oxford: Oxford University Press, 2016).

[13] Kidd, *America's Religious History*, 111.

[14] Other societies in the ancient Near East had similar laws; see the Laws of Hammurabi 14; the Hittite Laws 19–21; both in Martha T. Roth, *Law Collections from Mesopotamia and Asia Minor*, 2d ed. (Atlanta: SBL, 1997), 84, 220 (respectively).

[15] Wikipedia, "Slave Bible."

[16] *The Debates in the Several State Conventions, on the Adoption of the Federal Constitution, as Recommended by the General Convention at Philadelphia in 1787*, ed. Jonathan Elliot, 4 vols. (Washington: Printed for the Editor, 1836–1845), 4.316.

[17] William Harper, *Anniversary Oration, in the Representative Hall, Columbia, S.C., Dec. 9, 1835* (Washington: Duff Green, 1836), 9.

[18] Slavery was abolished in Massachusetts in the early 1780s when a state court determined, in the Quock Walker case, that the state constitution written by John Adams in 1780, with its statement that "all men are born free and equal," disallowed slavery.

[19] Aristotle, *Politics*, book 1. For an examination of ancient thoughts on slavery, see Garnsey, *Ideas of Slavery*. On Aristotle, see ch. 8, pp. 107–27. On the influence of Aristotle's idea that some people were born to be ruled, see ch. 3, pp. 35–52.

[20] E.g., the Parable of the Tenants (Mark 12:1–11); the Parable of the Talents (Matt 25:14–30).

[21] Instructions to slaves appear in Ephesians 6:5–9; Colossians 3:22–4:1; 1 Timothy 6:1–2; Titus 2:9–10; 1 Peter 2:18–21.

[22] Or, apparently that is what Paul is driving at, otherwise Paul may have seen himself as violating Deuteronomy 23:15–16, forbidding returning an escaped slave to his master. For a nuanced interpretation of Paul's intentions toward Onesimus, see John M. G. Barclay, "Paul, Philemon and the Dilemma of Christian Slave-Ownership," *New Testament Studies* 37 (1991): 161–86.

[23] Lenski, "Ancient Slaveries," 140–41; Hunt, *Ancient Greek and Roman Slavery*, 118–20. Manumission was much less common in the American South (Lenski, pp. 141–43).

[24] McCaulley, *Reading While Black*, 159, wonders how this passage would have been received in a Corinthian congregation composed in part of slaveholders and the enslaved.

[25] Garnsey, *Ideas of Slavery*, 181, comments: "In the Roman law of persons the fundamental division was between free men and slaves."

[26] According to Wendell Berry, *The Hidden Wound* (1970; Berkeley: Counterpoint, 2010), 15, Christian clergy were denied political power in Kentucky in the early nineteenth century in part because they kept attacking the institution of slavery. See also Berry's devastating portrait of what a southern American worship service must have involved in the nineteenth century and before, a worship service including slaves and their masters (pp. 16–19).

[27] See how Frederick Douglass takes up this point in his speech "What to the Slave Is the Fourth of July?" (1852), in

The Portable Frederick Douglass, ed. John Stauffer and Henry Louis Gates, Jr., (New York: Penguin, 2016), 195–222, at 212–18. In response to contemporary preachers who defended slavery from the Bible, Douglass (himself a Christian preacher) exclaimed, "welcome infidelity!"

[28] Alexander Campbell, "Tracts for the People—No. XXXIII. A Tract for the People of Kentucky," *Millennial Harbinger* (May 1849): 241–52, at 248.

Chapter 13

On Faith

Approaching Hebrews 11:1[1]

Now faith is the substance of things hoped for, the evidence of things not seen. (Heb 11:1, KJV)

So Dori looks at Marlin and says, "He says it's time to let go." Of course, Marlin doesn't believe her; not only is Marlin a naturally anxious fish, always worried about danger, but he's also learned that Dori is a fish that can't always be trusted. She's got ... issues. But in this predicament, inside a whale's mouth and holding on for dear life, Dori insists that she can understand the whale's speech, and she knows what they ought to do. They ought to let go. Marlin reluctantly acquiesces, and it turns out that Dori was right. Now, certainly, that scene in *Finding Nemo* (2003) is about overcoming anxiety, a good biblical theme (Matt 6:25–34), but it's also about trust. Marlin needed to trust Dori, trust that she had information that he didn't have (because she could speak whale), trust that her advice would result in success. It's a major theme of the movie, fear vs. faith, even faith in this hopelessly—well, not quite hopelessly—forgetful fish. Earlier, Dori had told Marlin that they needed to swim through a particular trench, not over it, advice to which Marlin strongly objected. Dori pleaded, "Come on, trust me on this." Marlin was incredulous: "Trust you?" Dori replied, "Yes, trust—it's what friends do." Here again, Marlin's trust, his faith, in Dori would have been well-placed, because Dori knew more about this trench than Marlin did.

Faith is about trust. It's about confidence in yourself or someone else. When I was a kid (and still pretty much today), I had complete confidence in my dad in a lot of situations. I knew if there was a problem, my dad would be able to solve it. Or, when it snowed in our southern town, I remember my dad wanting to get out and drive around town, see the blanket of white all over town, observe all the closed schools and businesses. Some people would have been nervous to drive in the snow, but not my dad, and I was not at all nervous about riding with him. I had confidence in him. I had faith that he could drive in snow.

God wants us to have faith in him. By some amazing circumstance—actually, we should call it amazing grace—that's pretty much all God wants from us. He knows we're not very bright, not very talented, pretty incompetent at most things. He doesn't expect much from us—just trust, faith, confidence in Him. Of course, that means that when He tells us to do something, He expects us to trust Him enough to do it. But it's not like He's told us to come up with a plan for saving the world. It's not like He expects us to do anything perfectly, or even very well. And let me say that you could get no better list of people who did not do things perfectly than the Faith Hall of Fame roll call in Hebrews 11. Nevertheless, these people show us faith. That's the whole point.

In fact, faith is such a defining element of what it means

to be a Christian that one of the most common ways of referring to Christians in the New Testament is "believers."[2]

What Is Faith?

How about some statistics? The Greek word for "faith" is
pistis (πίστις), which appears 243 times in the New Testament. But that's just the noun. The verb "I believe" is *pisteuō*
(πιστεύω), appearing 241 times in the New Testament, and
the adjective "faithful" (*pistos*, πιστός) appears another
sixty-seven times. If you're looking for these words in the
New Testament, it probably won't surprise you that you
should turn to Romans, which uses the noun forty times and
the verb twenty-one times; and John, which uses the verb
ninety-eight times (but never the noun); and Acts, which
uses the noun fifteen times and the verb thirty-seven times.

As for Hebrews,[3] the noun *pistis* appears thirty-two
times, of which twenty-four are in chapter 11.[4] Hebrews
uses the verb *pisteuō* only twice (4:3; 11:6), and the adjective
pistos five times (2:17; 3:2, 5; 10:23; 11:11).

Let me bring in one more element before moving off of
statistics. The Hebrew word most often associated with faith
is *emunah*, which appears most famously in Habakkuk 2:4
(where the Greek translation, the Septuagint, has *pistis*), the
verse quoted immediately before the Faith Hall of Fame
chapter (Heb 10:38). The other famous "faith" verse in the
Old Testament is Genesis 15:6, where the verbal form of
emunah is used (and the Septuagint has *pisteuō*).

Oh, yeah, and one more thing: the single word *pistis* can
cover all of the English words "faith" and "belief" and "faithfulness," all of which carry slightly different nuances in
English.[5]

What do these words mean?[6] Hebrews provides us with a definition, sort of. One of the problems is that Hebrews 11:1 is notoriously difficult to translate. Here are some options.

> Now faith is the substance of things hoped for, the evidence of things not seen. (KJV)

> Now faith is confidence in what we hope for and assurance about what we do not see. (NIV)

> Now faith is the assurance of things hoped for, the conviction of things not seen. (NASB, ESV)

> Now faith is the reality of what is hoped for, the proof of what is not seen. (CSB)

As you can tell, the translation issues really revolve around two words, which we can give in their Greek form this way.

> Now faith is the *hypostasis* (ὑπόστασις) of things hoped for, the *elenchos* (ἔλεγχος) of things not seen.

These words—*hypostasis* and *elenchos*—are not rare in Greek; it's the opposite problem: they occur quite a bit, with a range of meanings, so the difficulty is knowing which of their meanings is at play in our verse. We're not going to explore the meanings of these words in detail here, but we can take note of some recent discussions of them.

Teresa Morgan argues that *hypostasis* is best translated "foundation" here. According to Morgan, faith is foundational in that it creates our relationship with God (i.e. it is the foundation of our relationship). Faith is the foundation of things hoped for: it is the reason we can hope to achieve these things. As for the second half of the verse and the meaning of *elenchos*, "the likeliest meanings (which are all closely related to one another) are 'evidence', 'proof', or 'test'."[7] Morgan translates: faith is "the proof of everything (which God has promised) that [we] have not yet seen."[8] God has made promises to us about things that lie in the future—we have not yet seen them. Through faith, Morgan explains, "we come to prove the reality of what God has promised us and we hope for but have not yet seen: eternal life."

According to Nijay Gupta, "faith" in Hebrews 11:1 is a kind of spiritual sight,

> a kind of divinely enabled extrasensory perception, a second way of seeing and knowing. One can have confidence in what appears invisible—not because it is mere hunch or opinion, but because he or she has been given access to a perceptual key that unlocks a divine reality.[9]

And, of course, that key is faith, the trust that God knows things we don't know, has power we don't have, and loves us (i.e., exactly in accordance with Heb 11:6). So also Matthew Bates interprets faith here as "a willingness to act on God's more certain underlying reality (*hypostasis*) that is invisible yet visible through the manifestation of God's revealed word."[10]

The main point—a point we can get from this verse whether or not we know the precise nuances of each word—is that our faith is directed toward God, acknowledging that there are things for which we hope, things we cannot see, and yet we trust God, and such trust leads us to action.

That seems all very abstract. What does such faith look like in practice? That's what Hebrews 11 is all about. Such faith looks like Enoch and Noah and Abraham and Sarah and Moses and Rahab and Samuel. Most of all, it looks like Jesus (Heb 12:2). What all these examples show us is that *pistis* in Hebrews 11 includes trust, faithfulness, belief, confidence, obedience, and hope.[11]

The Life of Faith

The writer of Hebrews isn't just trying to fill out a certain number of pages; that's not why he goes through this list of examples. He's trying to motivate his readers to endure, to maintain their faith. These readers had apparently been Christians for a while, long enough that the writer now reminds them of the early days of their faith and how fervent their faith was (Heb 10:32). Back then, they endured persecution and had compassion on the oppressed (10:33–34). Now, perhaps, it was a different story, so that the writer admonishes, "you need endurance" (10:36). He reminds them of the things in which they hope, the promises of God (10:36), and then he quotes Habakkuk 2:3–4 (as Paul also does: Rom 1:17; Gal 3:11).

> For yet in a very little while
>> the one who is coming will come and will not delay;
>> but my righteous one will live by faith.
>> My soul takes no pleasure in anyone who shrinks
> back.

Our writer affirms: "But we are not among those who shrink back and so are lost, but among those who have faith and so are saved" (10:39).

In this way, the writer of Hebrews introduces his sustained reflection on the nature of faith, through illustrations of people who did not shrink back. These people were asked to do, sometimes, crazy things, and they did not shrink back. They faced hardship, and they did not shrink back. "All these died in faith without having received the promises, but from a distance they saw and greeted them" (11:13). We stand in the same position, looking forward to the promises, the things unseen, and refusing to shrink back.

Or is that too optimistic? Perhaps it would be more realistic to say that faith is disappearing all around us, that shrinking back is exactly what we are good at. Maybe when we reflect on what God wants us to do—the love and compassion and hope and joy and faithfulness that he wants us to demonstrate—we shrink back in fear and frustration, confident that we cannot possibly do such things.

Then, brethren, we need Hebrews 11. We need to read again the example of Rahab. We need to consider again the life of Samuel. We need to think about what Gideon was up against, and what he was able to accomplish "by faith." And most of all, we need to look to Jesus (Heb 12:2), as the writer of Hebrews emphasizes time and again.[12] There are other examples of faith in Scripture, as well—more mundane examples, less divine, less perfect, and the writer of Hebrews also highlights their faith so that they, too, can serve as examples to us. But Hebrews doesn't really stress the faith of Barak, or Rahab, or Gideon, or Enoch, or even Abraham or Moses. These characters come up here and there as examples of faith, but Jesus is everywhere. If you want to know about faith, look to Jesus.

***

Hebrews 11 encourages us not just to think about faith in the abstract but as something that must be enacted. That's the point of the great role call of faith. Look what faith led Enoch to accomplish! And Sarah and Moses and the rest! You can see it when someone trusts God, because their actions provide the evidence. We would not say that Marlin trusted Dori if he had not let go of that whale's tongue. We would not say that Joshua trusted God if he had not led the Israelites around the walls of Jericho for seven days (Hebrews 11:30). We would not say that David trusted God if he cowered in fear before the giant like King Saul and the rest of the Israelites (Heb 11:32; 1 Sam 17).

Trust God.

Endnotes

[1] This chapter first appeared in *Cloud of Witnesses: Ancient Stories of Faith*, Berean Study Series, ed. Ed Gallagher (Florence, AL: Heritage Christian University Press, 2020).

[2] For an exploration of the use of "believers" for Christians in the New Testament, see Paul Trebilco, *Self-Designations and Group Identity in the New Testament* (Cambridge: Cambridge University Press, 2012), ch. 3.

[3] Dennis R. Lindsay, "*Pistis* and *'Emunah*: The Nature of Faith in the Epistle to the Hebrews," in *A Cloud of Witnesses: The Theology of Hebrews in Its Ancient Contexts*,

ed. Richard Bauckham, et al. (London: T&T Clark, 2008),158–69, especially 160–61.

[4] The eight appearances of *pistis* in Hebrews outside chapter 11 are at 4:2; 6:1, 12; 10:22, 38, 39; 12:2; 13:7.

[5] For a discussion focused on the translation "faithfulness," see Matthew W. Bates, *Gospel Allegiance: What Faith in Jesus Misses for Salvation in Christ* (Grand Rapids: Brazos, 2019), ch. 2. Bates prefers "loyalty" or "allegiance" to "faithfulness" as a translation of *pistis*.

[6] The authoritative work here is Teresa Morgan, *Roman Faith and Christian Faith: Pistis and Fides in the Early Roman Empire and Early Churches* (Oxford: Oxford University Press, 2015). Morgan discusses Hebrews on pp. 330–41. See also Nijay K. Gupta, *Paul and the Language of Faith* (Grand Rapids: Eerdmans, 2020).

[7] Morgan, *Roman Faith and Christian Faith*, 338–41.

[8] Morgan, *Roman Faith and Christian Faith*, 340.

[9] Gupta, *Paul and the Language of Faith*, 10. See also Bates, *Gospel Allegiance*, 60, who denies that our verse promotes faith without evidence.

[10] Bates, *Gospel Allegiance*, 254–55n3.

[11] Morgan, *Roman Faith and Christian Faith*, 335.

[12] Todd D. Still, "*Christos* as *Pistos*: The Faith(fulness) of Jesus in the Epistle to the Hebrews," in Bauckham et al., *Cloud of Witnesses*, 40–50.

Section 3

The Church

Chapter 14

Why the Church?[1]

The church is the hope for the world. This bold assertion may strike many Christian readers as patently false—far from being the hope for the world; the church is everything that is wrong with Christianity. The church represents the institutional nature of Christianity, rules-based religion, and hypocrisy. Give me Jesus without the church! For Jesus is the one who is the hope for the world. He is the one who provides the perfect example of a life lived in service to God. He is the one who ate with sinners and welcomed prostitutes while chastising the hypocritical Pharisees. He is the one who sacrificed Himself on behalf of others, whose blood washes away sin. He is the one who conquered death, who ascended to the right hand of God, who always intercedes on our behalf. He is the one who left behind a community of followers to carry on His mission of turning the world upside down.

Aye, there's the rub. That community of followers that Jesus left behind is the church. If the church is the body of Christ, as Paul says on a number of occasions (e.g., 1 Cor

12:26; Col 1:18), then you cannot have Christ without the church. (That would be like Christ without Christ.) If the church manifests the kingdom of God in the world today, then it continues the mission of the one who came announcing that kingdom. If the church is a royal priesthood and a holy nation, as Peter thinks (1 Pet 2:9), then the world needs the church to be what God designed it to be. If God has planned the church from all eternity (Eph 1:4) and intended the church to reveal His "manifold wisdom" to "the rulers and authorities in the heavenly places" (Eph 3:10), then what does that mean for the importance of the church? The community Christ left behind shares His vocation of being a light to the nations (Isa 49:6; Matt 5:14), and bringing salvation to the ends of the earth (Matt 28:19). The church is the hope for the world.

The importance of the church in God's scheme of redemption becomes clear when studying Paul's interpretation of scripture. He continually interprets the Old Testament scriptures as finding their fulfillment in the communities that he is forming throughout Europe and Asia. When the law of Moses forbids muzzling a threshing ox (Deut 25:4), Paul insists that this commandment was written "altogether for our sake" (1 Cor 9:9–10). The story of Israel's sin with the golden calf (Exod 32) was "written for our instruction" (1 Cor 10:11; cf. Rom 15:4). Just as Christ fulfills the promise to Abraham of a seed (Gal 3:16; cf. Gen 22:18), so we who are in Christ are also Abraham's seed (Gal 3:29). One scholar has described this interpretive strategy as Paul's "ecclesiocentric hermeneutic," a hermeneutic centered on the church (ecclesia).[2] Paul sees much of the Bible as leading up to and foreshadowing the church.

Terminology

The Greek word *ekklēsia* signifies the assembly of believers, and many languages have taken their word for "church" from this word (cf. Latin *ecclesia*, French *église*, Spanish *iglesia*). The English language is different in this regard: the English word "church" derives not from *ekklēsia* but from a different Greek word, *kuriakon*, an adjectival form of *kurios*, meaning "lord" (a common description of Jesus or God in Greek). The adjective *kuriakos* appears a couple of times in the New Testament, once to describe the "lordly" supper (1 Cor 11:20), and another time to describe the "lordly" day (Rev 1:10). In the fourth century, the adjective could signify the "lordly" house, that is, the church building, as in the following example from the early church historian Eusebius:

> [The Roman Emperor Maximinus II] now allows [Christians] both to observe their form of worship and to build church buildings [*kuriaka*, plural of *kuriakon*].[3]

Here the word *kuriakon* simply means "church building." When the German tribes heard this word used for church buildings, they adopted it and applied it more broadly not only to the building but also to the institution, or the people who met in the building. The Germans bequeathed this word to the English, who made their own adjustments to the spelling and pronunciation, producing our word "church." But this word, "church," is now used as a translation of the New Testament word *ekklēsia*.

In the New Testament, the word *ekklēsia* appears 114 times, almost always referring to a Christian congregation or assembly. It does not have this meaning every time, such as in

Acts 19:40, where it refers to an "assembly" of a pagan mob. The word also appears in the Greek Old Testament—the Septuagint, commonly abbreviated LXX—one hundred times, usually in reference to the assembly of Israel (e.g., Deut 31:30).[4] A similar Greek term, *synagōgē*, appears even more often in the LXX, a total of 221 times (e.g., Lev 8:3). The two terms both mean "assembly" or "congregation," but by the first century it appears that the second of these terms, *synagōgē*, had taken on the meaning of a meeting place of Jews for Sabbath worship. Likely, it was this use of *synagōgē* that led the Jewish followers of the resurrected Messiah to avoid the term for their gatherings and prefer the other term that was prominent in the Greek version of Israel's scriptures, *ekklēsia*.[5]

Significance

The term "church" appears only three times in the Gospels, each time on the lips of Jesus in the Gospel of Matthew. This simple statistic makes it immediately clear that Jesus did not often speak about the church in those terms. Rather, He spoke of the kingdom of God, a phrase that appears 126 times in the Gospels (including related terminology, such as "kingdom of heaven"). But Jesus certainly did intend to form a community of believers who would embody His teachings and represent Him to the world after His departure. The concept of the church appears more frequently in Jesus's discourses than a simple count of the appearances of the term would indicate.

The two passages in which Jesus uses the term *ekklēsia* shed important light on the nature of the community envisioned by Jesus.[6] The first passage is the famous scene near

Caesarea Philippi when Peter first confesses that Jesus is the Christ (Matt 16:13–28). In response to this confession, Jesus says, in part, "I also say to you that you are Peter, and upon this rock I will build My church; and the gates of Hades will not overpower it" (v. 18). This verse has generated a great deal of discussion, especially in terms of the relationship between Peter and the rock.[7] Without entering deeply into the discussion, I would simply point out that Peter's confession may be the rock upon which the church is built, but even if the rock is intended to be Peter himself, the meaning would not diverge far from Paul's assertion that the apostles and prophets form the foundation of the church (Eph 2:20).

It is important to recognize two aspects of Jesus's use of the word "church" here. First, the word itself means "community" or "assembly." It is often said that "church" means the "called-out," but this is incorrect. While the word *ekklēsia* is formed by a prefix meaning "out" (*ek-*), and a lexeme meaning "called" (*klēsia*; cf. the verb *kaleō*), the compound term *ekklēsia* did not bear this significance, certainly not in first-century Greek. While Christians should be in some important ways separate from the world, we do not derive this teaching from the etymology of the word for "church."[8] Rather, *ekklēsia* means "community," and this, in itself, is of vast significance for the nature of the Christian life. Jesus did not envision individual Christian free agents, concerned merely with their own salvation and their personal relationship with God. In this passage, it is not the individual Christian who would carry on Christ's mission in the world. Jesus established a community, a group of believers who would work together, who would care for one another, who would jointly represent Christ. Jesus Himself gives the lie to the idea that one can have Christ without the church.

Second, the term *ekklēsia* connects the community established by Jesus with the community of Israel. One who reads the English Bible, beginning with Genesis, would not encounter the word "church" until Matthew 16:18, and thus might conclude that Jesus was introducing a brand new concept. But the disciples did not question Jesus about what He meant by this word "church." They knew precisely what an *ekklēsia* was because the term appeared frequently in their Scriptures in reference to the community of Israel. Jesus had come to form a renewed Israel, in line with Old Testament prophecies (e.g., Ezek 37:15–28; Jer 31:31). The new *ekklēsia* established by Jesus would be continuous with the people of God from the calling of Abraham forward.

The next time Jesus uses the word "church," He is addressing a procedure for dealing with a "brother" who sins (Matt 18:15–17). If this brother does not repent based on a personal conversation or, failing that, an intervention with a couple other believers, then the matter should come before the community (the church), and the community should attempt to persuade this brother. This text highlights the responsibility that the community bears for one another. This is no loose organization to which we can pay our annual dues and participate in if we choose. No, confessing Christ as Lord entails membership in a committed Christian community with the responsibility of helping other members of the community to maintain their faithfulness to Christ, and to accept their intervention on our behalf. Jesus intimated that His group of followers was a new type of family (Mark 3:31–35), and the term "brothers (and sisters)" is the most common designation in Paul's letters for Christians.

The community of Christ is to be as committed to one another as a family.

Almost always in Paul's letters (Ephesians and Colossians are exceptions), the term *ekklēsia* refers not vaguely to the church universal but concretely to the local congregation. This is where the rubber meets the road. The call of Jesus is a call to an actual assembly of flesh-and-blood people, with all their sins, annoyances, and folly, to be sure, but also with all their love, sacrifice, and goodwill. Whether we like it or not, Jesus has established His church, and He expects us to demonstrate a commitment to it as part of what it means to be committed to Him.

Endnotes

[1] This chapter first appeared in *The Ekklesia of Christ: Becoming the People of God*, Berean Study Series, ed. Ed Gallagher (Florence, AL: Heritage Christian University Press, 2019).

[2] See Richard B. Hays, *Echoes of Scripture in the Letters of Paul* (New Haven: Yale University Press, 1989).

[3] Eusebius, *Ecclesiastical History* 9.10.12.

[4] The Old Testament was originally composed in Hebrew. It was translated into Greek beginning in the third century BC. This Greek translation, the Septuagint, was often quoted in the New Testament and became the Old Testament for the early Greek-speaking Christians. It is still the Old Testament for the Greek Orthodox Church. See Gallagher, Edmon L. *The Translation of the Seventy: History, Reception, and Contemporary Use of the Septuagint* (Abilene, TX: Abilene Christian University Press, 2021)

[5] See Paul Trebilco, *Self-designations and Group Identity*

in the New Testament (Cambridge: Cambridge University Press, 2012), 164–207.

[6] It is unlikely that Jesus used the Greek word *ekklēsia* in his teaching. Jesus likely spoke Aramaic, and he probably used a corresponding Hebrew or Aramaic term, such as Hebrew *qahal* (Aramaic: *qᵉhēla*), which underlies each of the appearances of *ekklēsia* in the LXX.

[7] See, for instance, Joseph A. Burgess, *A History of the Exegesis of Matthew 16:17–19 from 1781 to 1965* (Ann Arbor: Edwards Brothers, 1976). See also Jack P. Lewis, "'The Gates of Hell Shall Not Prevail Against It' (Matt 16:18): A Study of the History of Interpretation," *Journal of the Evangelical Theological Society* 38 (1995): 349–67.

[8] For further reflections on the significance of the word church, see chapter 18 below.

Chapter 15

The Kingdom of God[1]

C hurches of Christ have long emphasized the close relationship between the kingdom of God and the church. Such an emphasis is entirely appropriate since the New Testament envisions the church and the kingdom in extremely similar terms.[2] Perhaps we have emphasized it a little too strongly, for Scripture does not present the kingdom of God as completely identical to the church; they are different concepts.[3] And yet, the church is the current earthly manifestation of the kingdom of God, the people who exhibit God's reign in the world now, who live within the kingdom even as they await its full revelation. If you are looking for evidence of God's kingdom today, the place to look is the church. Biblical teaching about the kingdom of God contributes to a better appreciation of the church's role within God's plan of salvation.

The first words out of the mouth of Jesus in the Gospel of Mark consist of an announcement that the kingdom of God would soon commence (Mark 1:15). Such an announcement would have been received by Jesus's contemporaries with, perhaps, a mix of anticipation (the oppressed crowds), trepidation (the political leaders), and disbelief (nearly everyone). For hundreds of years Judah had been dominated by foreign powers, from the Assyrians to the Babylonians to the Persians, Greeks, and now the Romans. While some first-century Jews no doubt longed for the time when God would establish His kingdom, others had probably long since ceased holding their breath.

The announcement by Jesus signaled the impending fulfillment of a variety of Old Testament promises. To be sure, God has always been king, and in that sense He has had a kingdom.[4] But the prophets had in varying ways envisioned a time when God would reign as king more fully and visibly than He currently did. The pivotal promise appears in 2 Samuel 7. God would establish David's dynasty, guaranteeing that one of his descendants would always reign over Israel (vv. 12–16). Through this "son of David" God would reign, for the son of David would also be the "son of God" (v. 14).

It quickly became apparent that the immediate descendants of David in no way lived up to the great promise of 2 Samuel 7. Though Solomon accomplished some great things (1 Kgs 3–10), he also oppressed the people (1 Kgs 12:4), promoted idolatry (1 Kgs 11:1–8), and indirectly caused the division of the kingdom into two separate nations (Judah and Israel) following his death (1 Kgs 12:1–15). And most of the other kings of Judah and Israel weren't even that good. Even while the Davidic dynasty was going strong, Isaiah longed for a time when "a shoot will spring from the stem of Jesse" (Isa 11:1). This new king from David's line— Jesse was David's father (1 Sam 16:1)—would bear the divine Spirit and would judge the people with righteousness, lifting up the poor and slaying the wicked (Isa 11:2–5). In his days there would be universal peace, even between animals and men, so much so that children need have no fear of poisonous snakes (vv. 6–9). The reign of this king would usher in a time of paradise, and God would reign through him.

Other prophets present their own visions of what it would look like when God reigns, when He establishes His kingdom. Ezekiel, a priest, imagines an enormous temple (chs. 40–48) from which flows a great river nourishing life-giving trees (47:1–12) and, most importantly, God Himself inhabits this temple (43:5). God will live among His people. Micah imagines God as a shepherd who would "assemble the lame and gather the outcasts" to be His kingdom (4:6–8). Sometimes in these visions of God's kingdom, the Gentile nations flock to Zion to learn God's will and join in worshipping Him (cf. Mic 4:1–3; Isa 2:2–4; cf. Isa 56:1–8; 60). Often it was imagined that twelve tribes of Israel would be regathered under one king, the new David (Jer 23:5–6; Ezek 37:15–28).

And so, though some people may have doubted the sanity of Jesus, no one could doubt His meaning when He declared that the time had finally arrived when God would begin to reign. Indeed, Jesus was the one through whom God would inaugurate His kingdom; He was the Messiah, as Peter and the apostles finally realized (Mark 8:29). When He cast out demons, the kingdom had come near (Luke 11:20). When He healed people of their diseases, He engaged in battle with the evil forces arrayed against God (Luke 13:16). He fought with Satan in the wilderness, and He overcame (Matt 4:1–11). His twelve chosen disciples (Mark 3:13–19) represented the regathered tribes of Israel (cf. Luke 22:30), just as He also attracted followers from roughly the geography of David's kingdom (Matt 4:23–25). He was the one, as Isaiah prophesied, on whom the spirit rested (Luke 4:16–21). He was the son of David whose throne would be established forever (Matt 1:1).

But He was different than what had been anticipated, and He spoke of a different kind of kingdom than what was expected. Not only was He David's son, but He was David's lord (Matt 22:41–46). In the kingdom preached by Jesus, blessings were pronounced on the poor in spirit, the merciful, the peacemakers (Matt 5:3–12). Jesus's kingdom was one that welcomed sinners (Mark 2:15–16; Luke 7:36–50) and prostitutes (Matt 21:31–32) and—worse yet—Gentiles (cf. Isa 2:2–4) while the most religious individuals were threatened with exclusion (Matt 8:11–12). This king, this expected one, who healed the sick and opened the eyes of the blind and preached the gospel to the poor (Matt 11:2–6), unexpectedly refused to proclaim Himself king openly (John 6:15; cf. Mark 1:24, 44; 3:11–12) and did not take up arms against Israel's enemy, Rome (Matt 26:52). Indeed, just the opposite: He allowed Himself to be mocked, tortured, and crucified by Rome. Certainly an odd type of king.

Yet the crucifixion was central to Jesus's notion of the kingdom. It was, after all, at the moment of crucifixion when Jesus received His royal crown (Mark 15:17) and hung under a sign proclaiming Him king (15:26). He had warned His disciples that this was going to happen (8:31; 9:31; 10:33–34) and that they themselves would have to do similarly (8:34). In Jesus's kingdom the first would be last (10:31) and the leaders would be servants (10:42–45; John 13:1–10).

The citizens of Jesus's kingdom would be characterized

by self-sacrifice (Matt 25:31–46), love (22:34–30), and commitment to one another (18:15–18). They would live by an elevated ethic, beyond normal interpretations of Moses' law (Matt 5:17–48). Not just adultery, but even lust was prohibited. Not just murder, but even hate was forbidden. Loving neighbors was fine, but citizens of this new kingdom would love their enemies. They would go the extra mile and turn the other cheek. They would do their righteous deeds to be noticed not by men but by God (6:1–18). They would trust God to provide their daily needs as they sought above all His kingdom (6:25–34). They would refuse to judge others but would walk the strait and narrow path (7:1–14). By living out the teachings of Jesus they would prove themselves worthy of entering the kingdom of heaven (Matt 7:21).[5]

When "all authority in heaven and on earth" has been given to Jesus following His suffering and resurrection (Matt 28:18)—that is, following His victory over death and the evil powers (Col 2:15; Heb 2:14–15)—clearly what Jesus has been announcing throughout His ministry has now come to pass: He is king, the kingdom of God has begun. If the kingdom does not appear as we might have guessed from the prophetic visions, Jesus Himself had cautioned us: only those who are born again can see the kingdom of God (John 3:3). Only renewed eyes of faith can discern the reign of God in the small group of Jews who stubbornly insist that someone crucified as a traitor had truly been and truly is the Messiah, the King in a newly established kingdom. When people accept this message and obey the teachings of Jesus the Messiah (Christ), God transfers them out of the kingdom of darkness and into the kingdom of His dear son (Col 1:13).

But the kingdom of God is not yet fully revealed. Jesus

inaugurated it but has not yet brought it to completion. We still pray for God's kingdom to come (Matt 6:10) because we long for the time when all creation will bow before Jesus and acclaim Him Lord (Phil 2:9–11; Rev 5:13). The church is an outpost of the kingdom of God now, a community already living under the rule of God in accordance with the ethic Jesus established, looking forward to inheriting the kingdom (Rom 8:17; cf. 1 Cor 6:9; 15:50) at the consummation of all things.

More than a century ago Alfred Loisy wrote, "Jesus announced the kingdom, and it is the church that came."[6] The church may seem a disappointment in comparison with the expectations created by Jesus's kingdom announcement. Perhaps such disappointment is in part due to the failure of Christians to embody the kingdom message of Jesus. The church ought to find its identity in "Jesus' vision of the kingdom of God and its instantiation in a community of disciples which already manifests, in the character of its life, the nature of God's coming universal rule."[7] Or, as Paul would have it, "the rule of God takes effect in the present in the fruit of the Spirit and in the gifts of the Spirit."[8] All too often in churches of Christ, it seems, we have equated the kingdom of God with the church—often in a battle against premillennialism—for the purpose of taming the kingdom, bringing it down to the normal, everyday level of the church. It would be more in keeping with Jesus's teaching to magnify the church as the present manifestation of God's kingdom, and therein find our mission and calling.

Endnotes

[1] This chapter first appeared in *The Ekklesia of Christ: Becoming the People of God,* Berean Study Series, ed. Ed Gallagher (Florence, AL: Heritage Christian University Press, 2019).

[2] See Scot McKnight, *Kingdom Conspiracy: Returning to the Radical Mission of the Local Church* (Grand Rapids: Brazos, 2014), who largely seeks to affirm the close relationship between church and kingdom.

[3] See Luke 12:32, where the community of Jesus (later to be called the church) would receive the kingdom, and so cannot be identical to it. The only passage that applies the label "kingdom" directly to the church is Revelation 1:6.

[4] For OT passages mentioning the kingship of God, see Psalms 47:2; 93:1; 95:3; 97:1; 98:6; 99:1; cf. 1 Samuel 8:7.

[5] On Matthew's peculiar use of the term "kingdom of heaven" rather than "kingdom of God," as in the other Gospels, see Jonathan T. Pennington, *Heaven and Earth in the Gospel of Matthew* (Leiden: Brill, 2007; Grand Rapids: Baker, 2009).

[6] Alfred Loisy, *L'Évangile et l'Église* (3d ed.; Bellevue: Chez l'auteur, 1904), 155 : "Jésus annonçait le royaume, et c'est l'Église qui est venue."

[7] Richard Bauckham, "Kingdom and Church According to Jesus and Paul," *Horizons in Biblical Theology* 18.1 (1996): 1–26, at 14.

[8] Bauckham, "Kingdom and Church," 16.

Chapter 16

The Israel of God[1]

That status of Israel as God's chosen people continues to stir and confuse both theological and political debate in our country. A great many Christians believe not only that God's plan for the end of the world involves the modern State of Israel in the Middle East, but also that God's promise to bless those who bless Abraham (Gen 12:3) requires that we support Israel. These Christians assert that modern Jews still constitute God's chosen people and that His promises to them of restoration and renewal must be literally fulfilled in them. At the same time, many Christians also think of America as a divinely chosen nation, a type of new Israel. Such political theology reaches back to before the founding of the nation (e.g., John Winthrop's "City on a Hill") and has only grown more prominent with the rise of evangelical Christians as a political force. In the early twenty-first century, love of country and love of God are so closely intertwined that one can hardly be a (conservative) Christian in America without also being a patriot.

However, these theological propositions demand close

scrutiny in the light of the New Testament teaching on the identity of Israel. After all, Israel is the one nation identified in the Bible as having been chosen by God. The Christian claim that modern Jews or modern America represent God's chosen people can receive validation only from the biblical teaching on the subject, as expounded in the Old Testament and brought to fulfillment in the New Testament. Especially noteworthy is Paul's blessing on the "Israel of God" in Galatians 6:16. This chapter will briefly discuss the meaning of this term and its implications for the church today.

Israel in Galatians

At the close of Paul's letter to the Galatians, he takes the pen from his secretary and writes with his own hand (6:11). To close this passionate letter in defense of the "truth of the gospel" (2:14), Paul wants to reiterate in his own handwriting some of the main points of what he had already dictated. To these churches being influenced to undergo circumcision as a requirement for being in a covenant relationship with God, Paul stresses that the Christian should not boast in the flesh but only "in the cross of our Lord Jesus Christ" (6:12–14). "For," he says, "neither is circumcision anything, nor uncircumcision, but a new creation. And those who will walk by this rule, peace and mercy be upon them, and upon the Israel of God" (6:15–16).

As this conclusion makes clear, Paul does not define the divinely recognized Israel according to physical characteristics. "For neither is circumcision anything, nor uncircumcision." In fact, later in his Letter to the Romans, Paul will say, "they are not all Israel who are descended from Israel" (Rom 9:6). Paul, then, makes clear that there are two different ways of conceiving of "Israel." One is according to circumcision, and one disregards circumcision. And it is the second way that defines the "Israel of God."

But if circumcision and physical descent do not set the boundaries for Israel, what does? Paul addresses this earlier in Galatians: "Even so Abraham believed God, and it was reckoned to him as righteousness [cf. Gen 15:6]. Therefore, be sure that it is those who are of faith who are sons of Abraham" (Gal 3:6–7). To be a "son of Abraham" does not require a physical link with the "Father of the Faithful," but rather faith itself creates the link. In Galatians, Israel is defined as those who have the faith of Abraham, regardless of ethnicity (cf. Rom 2:25–29).

The Mission of Israel in the Old Testament

Why is it important for Paul to identify believers with Abraham and Israel? Hasn't God done something completely new in establishing the church? Aren't his aims and purposes expanded now to the whole world rather than focusing on one small nation? This may be the way some of us think of the relationship between the Old Testament and the New Testament, but the statements from Paul that we have already examined indicate that he recognized a more intimate connection between what God was doing now in the church and what he has always been doing. Paul seems to be basing his view on what he perceives to be God's purposes for Abraham and Israel and the fulfillment of those purposes in the church. A brief exposition should clarify the matter.

The first eleven chapters of Genesis present a depressing picture of the beginning of the world. After God created everything and declared it all "very good" (Gen 1:31), sin and death quickly entered into the world in chapter 3 (cf. Rom 5:12; 1 Cor 15:20–22). While it seemed to start innocently enough with the eating of some forbidden fruit (Gen 3:1–7), it quickly escalated to murder (4:8, 23–24), so that by chapter six we read that "every intent of the thoughts of [man's] heart was only evil continually" (6:5). The initial transgression of Adam and Eve established that with sin came curse for the world (3:14–19), just as later Moses will tell the Israelites that the consequence of breaking the covenant entails a series of curses (Deut 27–28). God shows us that sin and curse cannot be permanently swept away with flood waters in Genesis 6–9, for as humans spread over the earth again following the flood, they take with them sin and curse (cf. 8:21).

In response to the problem posed by Genesis 1–11, God chooses a single family through whom would come blessing for the world. In Genesis 12:1–3, God selects Abram (who would become Abraham in Genesis 17:5) as the recipient of special promises. The last of these bears special import for our purposes: "And in you all the families of the earth will be blessed." Just as sin brought with it curse, now Abraham will bring with him blessing for the world (cf. Gal 3:8). Indeed, not just Abraham, but also his descendants; God repeats the promise later to Abraham (22:18), Isaac (26:4), and Jacob (28:14). Once we recall that Jacob would become Israel in Genesis 32:28, God's promise to bless all nations through Jacob/Israel takes on significance for God's calling of Israel to be his special people among all the nations of the earth (Exod 19:5–6). Israel would bring the blessing that would counteract the curse of sin.

God reveals His purposes for Israel clearly in the latter

part of Isaiah. As God's chosen servant (Isa 41:8–9; 44:18), Israel is appointed as "a covenant to the people" and "a light to the nations" (Isa 42:6). Yet, in this same section, God accuses Israel of failure: "Who is blind but My servant, or so deaf as My messenger whom I send?" (42:19) Instead of being a light to the nations, Israel had burdened God with sins (43:24). Israel had not kept the covenant, so upon them comes the curse of the Law—exile (Deut 28:58–68).

The Fulfillment of Israel's Mission

Even in Isaiah, God looks forward to a servant who would restore Israel and fulfill Israel's mission of being a light to the nations (49:1–6). Moreover, this servant would suffer for the sins of others (50:4–9; 52:13–53:12). So, in the fullness of time, a virgin gave birth to an Israelite boy in the town of Bethlehem, an Israelite who would not break the covenant, for he came for the purpose of fulfilling the Law and the Prophets (Matt 5:17). He suffered and died on a Roman cross, thus redeeming us from the curse of the Law (Gal 3:13). Paul's explanation of the purpose for which the Messiah suffered demonstrates the close relationship of the church to Abraham and Israel: "in order that in Christ Jesus the blessing of Abraham might come to the Gentiles, so that we would receive the promise of the Spirit through faith" (Gal 3:14). God had called Abraham, Isaac, and Jacob/Israel to bring blessing to all nations (Gentiles), and this blessing finally comes "in Christ Jesus."

Just as the ancient promises and covenant receive their fulfillment "in Christ Jesus," those who are "in Christ Jesus" by faith and baptism (cf. Gal 3:26–27) receive the blessings promised to Abraham instead of the curse resulting from sin.

This sheds some light on what Paul means by the term "Israel of God" at the end of the letter. Those of the faith of Abraham (3:7), those who are in Christ Jesus (3:14), are the ones who fulfill the covenant and receive the promises. These blessings come not as a result of physical descent and circumcision, but as a result of our identification through faith and baptism with the one who fulfilled the mission of Israel. In this way, we as believers in Israel's Messiah, as the church for which the Messiah died, become the Israel of God.

The "Israel of God" Today

Paul's identification of the "Israel of God" with the church has several implications for Christians in the twenty-first century. For, obviously, if the church is the Israel of God, then no other entity is the Israel of God, not even the modern State of Israel. This means that groups such as Christians United for Israel (CUFI), founded by prominent evangelical Pastor John Hagee, are off-base and promoting an ideology at odds with the New Testament. On their website (www.cufi.org), one can learn "Why Christians Should Support Israel." Much of what they argue has to do with pre-millenial expectation, but even more disturbing is their insistence that the promise of Genesis 12:3, that God will bless those who bless Abraham, entails that Christians should support the State of Israel. Have they not read Galatians? Israel is not defined by physical descent! Israel is not defined by circumcision! Rather, "it is those who are of faith who are sons of Abraham" (Gal 3:7)! The blessing of Abraham has come to the nations "in Christ Jesus" (3:14).

Perhaps maintaining close ties to the State of Israel benefits America politically, but Christians misunderstand their own identity when they assert these theological reasons for supporting Israel. As R. W. L. Moberly has written in his *Theology of the Book of Genesis*, such an interpretation of Genesis 12:3 "does not strike one either as particularly Christian or as displaying a grasp of the New Testament."[2] According to Paul, the church is the "Israel of God," and the blessings of Abraham have come to those who are in Christ Jesus.

Secondly, if the church is the Israel of God, then neither is America God's chosen nation to bring blessing to the world. When we read of God's relationship to Israel in the Old Testament, far too often we think that the relevant modern analogy is God's relationship to America, when in fact it is God's relationship to the church, the Israel of God. The stories in the Old Testament illustrate how God interacts with his chosen people, and the New Testament establishes that these are Christians.

Of course, in His providence, God may have plans for America, just as He may have plans for any nation founded by man. And yet, He has appointed a "holy nation" (1 Pet 2:9; cf. Exod 19:6) to accomplish His purposes in the world, and Christians deny their God-given responsibility when they look to political leaders to do the church's work. America's political system affords the opportunity for its citizens to take various roles in the governmental process, including voting for those leaders whom we feel represent our concerns; but, the church should not rely primarily on politics to execute its mission, which can be done regardless of who's in office. In campaign season (pretty much all the time) in which countless politicians will be promising salvation in one form or another—new jobs, strong defense, various social programs, etc.—Christians should remember that salvation can come to the world only through those for whom Christ died. America certainly offers great freedom and comfort resulting from a great deal of past and current sacrifice, and it has done much good in this world. Nevertheless, like Abraham of old, we look for a better country (Heb 11:16) and, like Paul, we realize that our citizenship is nowhere in this world (Phil 3:20).

Finally, as Christians—members of the church—the body of Christ—the Israel of God—we must, as Lincoln might say, take increased devotion to that cause for which Christ gave the last full measure of devotion. God chose Abraham and his descendants to bring blessing to the world, to undo the curse of sin. We are Abraham's descendants, if we are in Christ Jesus. God has not redeemed us from the curse of the law simply so that we may sit on a pew. He has assigned us a task, and it is time for the church to realize our identity as the Israel of God in Christ Jesus and bring the blessing of Abraham to all nations.

Endnotes

[1] This chapter first appeared in *Gospel Advocate* 156.3 (March 2014): 26–29.

[2] R. W. L. Moberly, *The Theology of the Book of Genesis* (Cambridge: Cambridge University Press, 2009), 176.

Chapter 17

Corporate Worship as Spiritual Discipline

In fact, we have arrived at a point now when the term "spirituality" is more apt to call to mind dabblers in transcendence than lives of rigor, exuberance, goodness, and justice—the kinds of lives historically associated with this word.[1]

The life of faith requires discipline. The same is true of any worthwhile endeavor: parents must discipline their children, athletes must discipline their bodies, students must discipline themselves to perform well in school, and Christians wishing to grow in their faithfulness to God must discipline their spirits. Being a good student does not happen without work. Being a faithful Christian—growing in one's imitation of Christ and love for other people, exhibiting more fully the fruits of the Spirit—does not happen without discipline.

Jesus provides the perfect example of one who was disciplined in terms of His spiritual life. His knowledge and understanding of scripture amazed His elders even while He remained very young (Luke 2:46–47). He continued to draw from scripture throughout His ministry (Luke 4:18–19; 24:27), even in ways that frustrated and confounded His opponents (Matt 4:1–11; Mark 12:24, 35–37). Such intimate acquaintance with scripture surely reflects frequent study and meditation by Jesus. He also reserved time to pray, whether early in the morning (Mark 1:35) or during troubling times (Mark 14:32–42). Jesus worshipped regularly, frequently appearing in synagogues (Matt 4:23; Mark 1:21; 3:1; Luke 4:16). Each of these disciplines contributed to His "increasing in wisdom and stature, and in favor with God and men" (Luke 2:52).

These same practices should give shape and substance to the spiritual lives of Christians today. Here I especially want to emphasize the spiritual discipline derived from regular participation in the public worship of the church. In some ways, simply the act of meeting together with the church each Sunday is a discipline that leads to spiritual maturity. Joining with other Christians each Lord's Day encourages us to love each other more intimately, and seeing fellow disciples striving to live righteously and please God inspires us to do the same.

Let's not sugarcoat the Christian assembly. If I'm being honest, I love not going to church. That was one aspect of the pandemic that I enjoyed (as I mention also in the next essay). And when I was young, staying home from church on Sunday night or Wednesday night because I was sick or whatever meant that I got to watch Punky Brewster or other TV shows I usually couldn't see. It was wonderful. There's an analogy with exercise: today, in my 40s, I do not enjoy running. I do it because it's good for me. When it comes to church attendance, I'm not completely impious: I enjoy going to church more than I enjoy running. The point I'm trying to make right now is that being a part of the community of God's people, rather than a solo Christian, is good for me, and I need to do it whether I really want to or not. The simple act of gathering with other people, putting it on the schedule, making it part of the weekly routine, aids spiritual growth—precisely because it gets you in the habit of squashing some of your own desires.

And then there's what we do when we get together. Most of the time that involves worship. Here again, we do not perform these actions merely because God told us to, or because we need to check those boxes to stay on the right side of God, or even because we enjoy them. And sometimes —maybe not often enough, but sometimes—we do enjoy these actions of corporate worship; sometimes our united singing moves us in unexpected ways, or the words of a prayer express thoughts we didn't realize we had, or a sermon punches us in the gut in just the way we need, or it introduces us to exciting possibilities. But we perform these actions not just for those reasons, but also because they are good for us, because they discipline us in holiness, in life with God.

Traditionally in churches of Christ we have talked about five particular acts of worship: singing, praying, reading Scripture, giving, and communion (Lord's Supper). Though Scripture does not provide a list of these actions as such, it does mention each of these elements in the context of New Testament worship. We should approach these acts not as requirements that must be fulfilled before we leave the assembly, but as disciplines through which we mature in our spirit, as opportunities for us to grow closer to God. Let's think about them one-by-one.

I

When we sing we proclaim the goodness of God and his rich blessings toward us, and we declare our allegiance to him above all other masters in this world. We have plenty of examples in Scripture; think about the Psalms, which can be considered an instruction manual for approaching God in song and prayer. The Psalms contain more than just praise—in fact, there are more lament psalms in the Psalter than any other type of psalm.[2] But praise they do contain, and the church's ministry of singing is often focused on praise, so it may be helpful to think Scripturally about praise specifically. (We may also learn from the Psalter that we need more periods of communal lament.) In an essay advancing several theses regarding praise in the Psalter, Walter Brueggemann mentions two that I find especially helpful: praise is an act of doxological self-abandonment, and praise is a polemical act.[3]

First, doxological self-abandonment. Think about that term and how it describes the ideal of singing praise to God. We spend most of our lives caring for ourselves: eating, or exercising, or getting money, or spending money, or entertaining ourselves, watching TV or going on vacation or whatever. The typical human life is pretty much a life of self-absorption, even for Christians, even though the call of Christ is to deny ourselves (Luke 9:23). Singing gives us the opportunity to remove the focus from ourselves, our needs, our desires, and redirect our hearts toward God. It is an opportunity to abandon ourselves in doxology, praise of God. Never are we more truly human—more reflecting the divine image—than when we engage in doxological self-abandonment. Beyond the psalms, think about the scene in Revelation 4, when the four living creatures flying around the heavenly throne room chant, "Holy, holy, holy, Lord God Almighty, which was, and is, and is to come," while the twenty-four elders fall before the One sitting on the throne and throw their crowns at His feet proclaiming, "Thou art worthy, O Lord, to receive glory and honour and power: for thou hast created all things, and for thy pleasure they are and were created." In the presence of God, it seems impossible to be concerned with one's own needs or desires, but one finds fulfillment only in magnifying God. Doxological self-abandonment.

Praise is also a polemical act. Polemics is about warfare, fighting, battle. A polemical act is an aggressive act, an act of warfare. There is no more polemical book in the New Testament than Revelation, in which the dragon (Rev 12) and the beast (Rev 13) and the harlot (Rev 17) are the major enemies of God's people. Indeed, we find that the beast from the sea receives worship from people (Rev 13:4), and he is joined by another beast, one from the earth, whose job it is to compel people to worship the sea beast (13:12) and to signal their allegiance by receiving a mark constituting the beast's name (13:16–18). Doesn't this context significantly raise the stakes of the type of praise offered in chapter 4? "Thou art worthy, O Lord, to receive glory and honour and power"—and not the beast! A polemical act.

In our praise, we announce to the world—sometimes as loud as we can shout (a war cry)—that we serve a living God, all-powerful, creator of the heavens and the earth. Other "gods" try to get our attention, but we worship only one God. We sing words like "All to Jesus I surrender." These are the weapons of our warfare, which are not merely fleshly weapons like swords or guns, but our weapons have divine power to destroy strongholds. "We take every thought captive to obey Christ" (2 Cor 10:5).

Again, let's not sugarcoat it. The words of our praise songs, such as "All to Jesus I surrender," rarely accurately reflect our hearts. Do we actually surrender everything to Jesus? Is that what an outside observer would say about our lives? It may be—and probably is—that during the previous week we have not surrendered all things to Jesus. It may be that we have exalted other things (family, work, pleasure) over Jesus. It may be that the words of the song do not accurately reflect our lives. But that does not mean that we should stop singing the song. No! We must sing it. We must transform our hearts by singing this song, so that we dedicate our lives to making true the words that we sing. Our songs can challenge us to live up to the standards of the words that our mouths proclaim. And when we sing "Fairest Lord Jesus" or "How Great Thou Art," and at the same time we dedicate our hearts to these songs, we discipline our spirits to conform to these powerful words.

II

Now we turn to prayer, and we know that it is a useless act—which is the very reason we must do it. I don't mean that it's useless in the sense that we're really talking to no one, or that even if there is a God, He doesn't actually respond to our prayers. I don't mean that at all. I mean that prayer is useless in the sense that it takes time away from our busy lives and does not help us accomplish anything. We don't have time for prayer. Our lives are filled to overflowing with activities, work, even church responsibilities. We can just squeeze in the events required for the day, sometimes;

often we have to let certain things slip away undone. Can we really afford to take time out of that packed schedule to sit there and talk to someone—who, after all, already knows everything we're going to say, as our Lord assures us (Matt 6:8)? Prayer is useless; it doesn't help us get anything done, and we feel the constant pressure to get things done.

Do you remember that old joke about the preacher who went into the office one weekday morning and told the secretary that he was not to be disturbed for the next hour because he was going to pray? The secretary said he could not spend an hour in prayer because his day was booked solid; he had an unusual number of meetings and other things to do. The preacher's response? "Oh me, you're right, I'm going to need to spend two hours in prayer!" If that joke is funny at all, it's because it seems simultaneously ridiculous and profound. The secretary is thinking straight: an hour of prayer is not going to help the preacher get through all the scheduled activities of the day. And the secretary is not thinking Christianly enough, because when we imagine that so much depends on our activity, prayer is exactly what we need to reorient us lives toward God, who holds all things in his hand.[4]

I love the way Pete Greig puts it in his book, *How to Pray*:

> There are definitely days I'd prefer a set of personal superpowers to slogging away at the slow, confusing business of prayer. God knows that we don't always find it easy to string a sentence together in his presence. "He remembers," as the psalmist says, "that we are dust" (Psa 103:14). He understands that we sometimes get tongue-tied, distracted, overwhelmed, and confused. He doesn't

get insecure if we occasionally doubt his existence. He sees our bruised and broken hearts and accepts that prayer hasn't always seemed to help. He isn't in the least bit annoyed that we occasionally find talking to him a bit boring. Or that we would sometimes prefer to scale the Empire State Building covered in spandex than merely, meekly to "go into [our] room, close the door and pray to [our] Father, who is unseen" [Matt 6:6].

But the thing is this: *He likes us.* A lot.[5]

Later in the same chapter, Greig makes an essential point:

I don't want to put anything heavy or unsustainable on you as you seek to grow in prayer. But here is the great and inescapable truth—taught in Scripture, modeled by Christ, and advocated without exception by all the heroes of our faith: You cannot grow in prayer without some measure of effort and discomfort, self-discipline and self-denial.

All that I've said so far concerns prayer in general, which is a *sine qua non* of spirituality. But now let's think specifically about corporate prayer. After all, as Andrew McGowan reminds us,

Prayer for the first Christians involved far more than forming and expressing individual ideas or words; it was profoundly communal as well as highly personal, and a matter of body as well as mind.[6]

When someone leads a prayer in public worship, and we

pray silently along with that person, the effect can be much like the singing. The prayer leader says words that may not reflect our own lives. He thanks God for the blessings of life, when we may want to attribute our blessings to our own hard work. He thanks God for saving us from our sins, when we probably do not want to think about our sins and our need for God's salvation. He asks God to lead our lives, when we may prefer to direct our own steps. He asks God to deliver us from evil, when we may want to give in to temptation. But as we pray along with this public prayer, if we think about the prayer as a spiritual discipline, it will help us to live the holy life to which we have been called.

III

Scripture has always formed a central aspect of Christian gatherings.[7] But the Bible is often not easy to understand. Sometimes people get this fact confused. It's the gospel that is easy enough for a kindergartner to understand, at least at a very basic level. The gospel is not the Bible; it is reported in the Bible, but the two are not the same. There are parts of the Bible that are easy enough to understand—again, at a basic level. The stories in the Gospels for instance, or Acts, or Samuel. But there is also plenty of material in the Bible that is not easy at all. We could think about those passages that are just difficult to figure out any meaning, such as Paul's comment that "all Israel will be saved" (Rom 9:26), or Daniel's prophecy of the Seventy Weeks (Dan 9:24–27), or Jesus's Parable of the Unrighteous Steward (Luke 16:1–9), or quite a bit in the book of Revelation. Beyond those passages, we can think about the passages, perhaps even more difficult, that seem easy enough to understand but apparently say things that seem out of harmony with Scripture as a whole, such as God's command to Abraham to sacrifice his son (Gen 22), or Paul's statements on slaves and masters (Eph 6:4–9). I often compare passages of Scripture to mathematics: certain passages are arithmetic, relatively simple, and other passages are calculus, requiring much more study and contemplation.

There's the point. Why did God give us Scripture that is often so difficult to grasp? It requires study and contemplation. We could ask the same question regarding the favorite teaching method of Jesus; in fact, the disciples did ask that question: "Why do you speak to them in parables?" (Matt 13:10). We can imagine the thought that the disciples are not bold enough to express to Jesus: "No one knows what you're talking about!" The response of Jesus reveals that that's exactly the way He wants it. Far from parables making things easier to understand, Jesus uses parables specifically because they hide their meaning. "The reason I speak to them in parables is that seeing they do not perceive, and hearing they do not listen, nor do they understand" (Matt 13:13, reflecting the commissioning statement of Isa 6:9–10). What could Jesus possibly mean? He doesn't want people to understand? He doesn't exactly explain Himself, but I imagine what He's getting at is that He wants people to work for the meaning. He doesn't want to spoon-feed them all the time. He wants to challenge the crowds to seek so that they may find, to knock before the door is opened—not just to walk through an already open door. Where's the growth in that? Scripture is hard because God wants us to wrestle with its meaning. That's part of our spiritual growth.

And when we study and contemplate Scripture, what we learn is that Scripture is not primarily about me. I think this is where a lot of Christians get hung up. They want the Bible always to speak to their immediate needs, to have a word that is immediately applicable to them. But, again, it's sorta like math, or whatever other area of study you prefer. There is an immediate application for calculus; there are items we use everyday that require calculus, but it's not the kind of thing that you're going to be able to perceive on your first day of math class. It takes a lot of training to get to the point where you can see the immediate application. When it comes to Scripture, we must realize that I am not the main character but rather God is. Scripture wants to reveal to us our God. There are passages that do not seem immediately relevant to me, but they are immediately relevant to God, to telling me what kind of God I serve. That is the relevance. The exposition of Scripture in our corporate worship reminds us of our place in God's world.

IV

Taking up a collection is less obviously a part of earliest Christian corporate worship than are the other things we are discussing,[8] and in some congregations today, passing the baskets is on its way out as churches promote online giving as both a convenience to members and as a better source of revenue, since automatic online contributions are automatic, not subject to forgetfulness or vacations. Sometimes automatic online giving is promoted by church leaders as a positive thing because the church member no longer has to think about giving at all. I think that means that giving has been demoted from an act of worship to merely a way to pool our resources. Have we lost something? Is there any value in thinking of giving as an act of worship? Let me see if I can convince you.

> Yahweh is king! Let the earth rejoice;
>> let the many coastlands be glad!
>> ...
>> All worshipers of images are put to shame,
>> those who make their boast in worthless idols;
>> all gods bow down before him.
>> Zion hears and is glad,
>> and the towns of Judah rejoice,
>> because of your judgments, O God.
>> For you, O Yahweh, are most high over all the earth;
>> you are exalted far above all gods. (Ps 97:1, 7–9)

Psalm 97 reminds us of the point we explored earlier in regard to singing, that praise is a polemical act. We exalt our God and not any other god, not any worthless idol, because our God loves us and provides for us and redeems us—all things of which idols are incapable. And yet the world is full of idols, and perhaps the most attractive to us is money—that green idol bearing the image of someone who is not our God. You will remember, of course, that it was precisely greediness that Paul labeled idolatry (Col 3:5). And you will recall that Jesus declared it impossible to serve two masters; we must choose between God and Mammon (Matt 6:24). Passing the baskets on a Sunday morning allows us as God's people the opportunity to publicly declare that we choose God. It is a moment when we rid ourselves of Mammon, untangle ourselves from the weeds distracting us from who we really are (Matt 13:22). Like singing, putting our money into the basket is a polemical act. (Does automatic online giving allow the same opportunity?) It is an act of non-conformity, as the apostle urges (Rom 12:2). When people routinely post to their feeds the pictures of their fabulous and expensive vacations or their new cars or whatever, we are encouraged to bow down to Mammon. When the basket comes around on Sunday morning, we are encouraged to forsake Mammon in favor of the one alone who can fulfill our needs. When approached in this way, the contribution is an important act of worship that aids in our spiritual formation.

V

The Lord's Supper is a rich symbol that can have a variety of meanings. One of its least appreciated meanings is its call to us to imitate our Master's sacrifice. Paul criticizes the Corinthian practice of taking the Lord's Supper because the Christians in Corinth were focusing on themselves and not on other people (1 Cor 11:17–34). The Lord's Supper was instituted by Jesus to remind us of His self-sacrifice. "This is my body that is for you," Jesus said—for you, not for Himself (11:24). "This cup is the new covenant in my blood" (11:25), or, in another telling, "This is my blood of the covenant, which is poured out for many" (Mark 14:24). Jesus poured out His blood for others. That's what we remind ourselves when we drink that juice. Indeed, "as often as you eat this bread and drink this cup, you proclaim the Lord's death until he comes" (1 Cor 11:26). Did you catch that? The death of the one we call "Lord." The self-sacrifice of the one to whom we give our allegiance. When we eat the bread and drink the cup, we claim to be followers, imitators, of the

Master who made Himself a slave. Do we really want to imitate that?

Paul says that it is possible to eat the bread and drink the cup of the Lord "in an unworthy manner" so that one is "guilty of the body and blood of the Lord" (11:27). This will happen if the worshipers fail to "examine" themselves (11:28), which would result in eating and drinking "judgment against themselves" (11:29). Instead, one must "discern the body." Paul does not explain how to "discern the body" or even what "body" he means, but in context it makes sense that he means "the body of Christ"—not the body that hung on the cross but the body that is composed of God's people (1 Cor 12:27). If we do not "discern the body" or think correctly about the people of God who together with us form Christ's body, we bring judgment on ourselves. What should we do? We should imitate our Lord and be willing to sacrifice ourselves on behalf of others. Or else, what? We eat and drink judgment on ourselves.

Think of it this way: if the bread and the juice are supposed to remind us of Jesus—"do this in remembrance of me"—and we are supposed to think especially of His self-sacrifice for others, and we eat this bread and drink the cup while also refusing to imitate Jesus in His self-sacrifice for others, is such worship pleasing to God? Or is it more likely that He would respond in the words of Amos 5:21, "I hate, I despise your festivals."

Let me turn the screws just a little further. Read the Parable of the Unforgiving Servant (Matt 18:23–35). That's the one where the one servant owes a ton of money to his master and receives incredible grace in the form of forgiveness of his debt, though this servant is himself unwilling to forgive the much smaller debt of his fellow servant. That stinginess on the part of the servant angered the master immensely. The point: the master expected—required, even —the forgiven servant to imitate the master's forgiveness (see also Matt 6:14–15). Now, think about someone you don't like. Consider what this parable requires of you in regard to this person. Are you willing to do what your Lord requires? When you eat the body and drink the blood of your Lord, you proclaim to the world, and to yourself, and to God in heaven, that you are once again committing yourself to become like Christ. That little piece of bread and that small cup of juice represents your submission to the will of another. Are you willing to submit? Are you willing to obey? You who have been forgiven, are you willing to forgive? Decide before you eat the bread and drink the cup, or you will be guilty of the body and the blood of the Lord.

The Lord's Supper is certainly about remembering Jesus, but it is also about becoming like Jesus. And that is the point of all spiritual discipline.

***

The public worship of the church is one of the most important Christian spiritual disciplines that itself encompasses a range of disciplines. Corporate worship does not replace private devotion, including Bible reading and prayer, but meeting together with the saints is something that not only God expects but that is essential for our own spiritual development. Worshipping God regularly with other Christians and thinking about the acts of worship in which we participate will help us to live disciplined lives in imitation of our Lord.

Endnotes

[1] Eugene H. Peterson, *Eat This Book: A Conversation in the Art of Spiritual Reading* (Grand Rapids: Eerdmans, 2006), 16.

[2] For a helpful analysis of the types of psalms, see Walter Brueggemann's seminal essay, "Psalms and the Life of Faith: A Suggested Typology of Function," *Journal for the Study of the Old Testament* 17 (1980): 3–32, reprinted in *The Psalms and the Life of Faith*, ed. Patrick D. Miller (Minneapolis: Fortress, 1995), 3–32. Brueggemann classifies the psalms according to whether they represent orientation, disorientation, or reorientation.

[3] Walter Brueggemann, "Praise and the Psalms: A Politics of Glad Abandonment," *The Hymn* (October 1992), reprinted in *The Psalms and the Life of Faith*, 112–32. I am reflecting on Brueggemann's sixth and seventh theses, which he discusses on pp. 116–18.

[4] You might want to look back at chapter 2 on Elijah, which explores some of these same ideas.

[5] Pete Greig, *How to Pray: A Simple Guide for Normal People* (Carol Stream, IL: NavPress, 2019), ch. 2.

[6] Andrew B. McGowan, *Ancient Christian Worship: Early Church Practices in Social, Historical, and Theological Perspective* (Grand Rapids: Baker, 2013), 184. See McGowan's whole chapter for a demonstration of this point.

[7] See McGowan's relevant chapter, *Ancient Christian Worship*, 65–110.

[8] For instance, McGowan, *Ancient Christian Worship*, has no chapter on the collection.

Chapter 18

A Worshiping Community on a Mandated Break[1]

The pandemic has been bad for me: I've enjoyed it too much.

Well, I have not actually enjoyed the pandemic so much as the decree to avoid people, to stay home. As an introvert, a father for a homeschooling family, a teacher who has for years earned a living from online education, I found myself largely unaffected by government-mandated lockdowns. Actually, such mandates proved to be a period of refreshment, relaxation for me and my family. True, we live in deep-red Alabama, where there is no discernible panic about the pandemic, and an actual lockdown lasted for only a couple weeks. But to the extent that we could use the pandemic as an excuse to stay home, we were living the high life. Our time had come.

And I suffered—not any sort of emotional distress or other felt pain, but an enhancement of my own negative qualities. Just as Ilsa could not stay with Rick but had to get on that plane with Victor—otherwise she would regret it, maybe not today, maybe not tomorrow, but someday, and for the rest of her life—so also my yielding to my own moderately negative tendencies to avoid people (like the priest and Levite mentioned by Jesus; Luke 10:31–32)[2] has led me further from Jesus, further from the one who magnified love of neighbor as one of the twin pillars upholding the entire Law and the Prophets (Matt 22:40), further from the one who expressly commanded his disciples to follow his example of self-effacing service to others (John 13:15), further from the one who pronounced such service a chief criterion of judgment (Matt 25:31–46).

The pandemic has been bad for me. Whether I like it or not, I need the church.

***

It is not good that the man should be alone.
　　—Genesis 2:18

God's plan has always been for people to live in community. As Christian psychologist Mark Yahrhouse proposes: "To be human is also to experience a longing for completion."[3] Or C. S. Lewis: "We are born helpless. As soon as we are fully conscious we discover loneliness. We need others physically, emotionally, intellectually; we need them if we are to know anything, even ourselves."[4] Lewis was talking about what he called Need-love and later came to call Affection (which he linked to the Greek term *storge*), the kind of love indicative of parents and children but seen also in other relationships. Marriage or family is one way of satisfying the human need for companionship. According to Jesus, Christian believers form a family, the bonds of which transcend other family ties that are based on blood or legal contract

(Mark 3:31–35). Our Lord asserted that there might be times when abandoning traditional family units could accomplish God's will and lead to the establishment of stronger and more numerous family relationships (Mark 10:29–30). He even proclaimed the necessity of "hating" (Luke 14:26)—or, at least, "loving less" (Matt 10:37)—traditional family members on behalf of Jesus. On more than one occasion Paul says that Christians have been adopted by God, so that they can now address God as "Father" (Rom 8:15–17; Gal 4:5–6). The most common label for Christians in the New Testament is, of course, not "Christians" or even "disciples," but "brothers (and sisters)."[5] If it is not good for the man to be alone, the New Testament encourages us to think that the primary way for God's children to find companionship is not in a traditional family but in God's family.[6]

While the New Testament usually calls individual believers "brothers (and sisters)," it usually refers to the family to which they belong by the label *ekklesia* (ἐκκλησία). This word appears 114 times in the New Testament and a hundred times in the Greek Old Testament (of which 23 occurrences are in the deuterocanonical portions). In the New Testament, Paul uses the term far more than other writers (62 times in the thirteen canonical letters), though it also appears frequently in Acts (23x) and Revelation (20x). In the rest of the New Testament, the word is "patchily distributed" (Matt, 3x; Heb, 2x; James, 1x; 3 John, 3x).[7]

How shall we translate *ekklesia*? Traditionally, in English, we use the word "church" in translations of the Bible,[8] but only in contexts in which the Christian community is in view. There are contexts, even in the New Testament, when the Christian community is not in view (Acts

7:38; 19:32, 39, 40).[9] Clearly the word "church" is not always appropriate, even in the New Testament. Is it ever appropriate? Though "church" is traditional in the English Bible, the first major English Bible translator to base his work on the Greek and Hebrew texts rejected it. William Tyndale used "congregation" as a translation of *ekklesia*, thinking that "church" carried too much baggage having to do with hierarchy and institutionalism.[10] The current standard Greek-English lexicon for the New Testament (BDAG) agrees with Tyndale, suggesting the glosses "assembly" or "gathering" or "community" or "congregation," reserving the gloss "church" only for those instances that have a worldwide entity in view.[11]

We have noted that *ekklesia* appears a hundred times in the Greek Old Testament (e.g., Deut 31:30), though we never in our English Bibles encounter the word "church" before Matthew. The two main words in Hebrew that denote the congregation of God are *qahal* (123x) and *ēdah* (149x). In the LXX, *qahal* often (73x) becomes *ekklesia*, but also often (35x) *synagoge* (συναγωγή). *Ēdah* is usually translated *synagoge* (130x), never *ekklesia*. Thus, at the time of Jesus the Greek Scriptures contained two prominent words for the community of God, both meaning basically the same thing, but one of them had already become associated with Jewish synagogues. This prior adoption of the most prominent term in the LXX (in which *synagoge* appears 221x) may have contributed to the Christian adoption of the second most prominent term in Scripture for their gatherings.[12]

Though *ekklesia* appears mostly in Paul and hardly at all in the Gospels, it does appear on the lips of Jesus in two passages in Matthew. Most famously, Jesus responded to

Peter's confession of faith in his Messiahship by promising to build his *ekklesia*, which would not be overcome by the gates of Hades (Matt 16:18). In the English Bible, this verse is the first occurrence of the word "church," but in the Greek Bible the word *ekklesia* has already appeared a hundred times (or 77 times, if the deuterocanonicals are excluded). So we see at least a few significant obstacles that the translation "church" poses for Christian readers: the English word itself, as Tyndale insisted, carries connotations that have little to do with *ekklesia*. Moreover, such a translation obscures the connections between the assemblies of God scattered throughout the Mediterranean world in the first century, and the assembly of God about which these Christians read in their ancient Scriptures. As the previous sentence already indicates, a better translation would be "assembly," as scholars (noted previously) widely recognize.

But "assembly" itself is not without problems. Does such a term intimate that the group ceases to exist when not assembled? That is indeed the case for an *ekklesia* in fifth-century BC Athens, where the term meant something like "public meeting officially summoned," as the *Cambridge Greek Lexicon* puts it.[13] The *ekklesia* no longer existed once the assembly was dismissed. The same usage is indicative of the LXX for the most part, but some passages such as Deuteronomy 23 (prohibiting certain categories of people from entering the *ekklesia* of the Lord; cf. Neh 13:1) evince a more permanent existence of the *ekklesia*, beyond any actual meeting.[14] The same is true of Philo—and Paul.[15] As Andrie Du Toit has shown, Paul sometimes uses *ekklesia* for an actual meeting (1 Cor 11:18; 14:19, 28, 34, 35), but more often he uses the word for a group of Christians that sometimes meets together (e.g., Rom 16:1). Aside from these two meanings, Du Toit also allows that Paul may sometimes have in view the universal church—that is, a worldwide society that could never actually assemble—a concept more clearly in play in some of the disputed Pauline letters.[16] If "assembly" does not properly capture Du Toit's second and third definitions, what is the better term? Tyndale chose "congregation," which perhaps can refer to a group that outlasts its congregating. "Community"—one of the definitions offered by BDAG—might be even better.

One thing *ekklesia* does not mean is "called out," at least, not in the sense proposed by a popular explanation of the word.[17] To be sure, the etymology of the word does imply this meaning (*ek*, "out"; *klesia*, "called"), and one can imagine the citizens of Athens being "called out" of their various locations so that they might assemble. But etymology is not related directly or intuitively to the meaning of a word. (Think: driveway and parkway, or manufacture.) Usually, when people link *ekklesia* to the meaning "called out," they intend to urge Christians to be separated from the dominant thought processes of the world. It is true that in some important ways Christians should be separate from the world, but we do not derive this idea from the etymology of *ekklesia* but rather from explicit New Testament teaching: "They do not belong to the world, just as I do not belong to the world" (John 17:16); "be not conformed to this world" (Rom 12:2).[18] The earliest Greek-speaking Christians used the word *ekklesia* for their gatherings and communities not because of its etymology but because it means "community" and especially because they found the word in their Scriptures in reference to the people of God.

The importance of the *ekklesia* as "community" can be seen throughout the New Testament, in the metaphors for

God's people (e.g., body of Christ; temple of God), in the ecclesiocentric Scriptural interpretation of Paul and other New Testament writers,[19] and in the second (and final) passage in the New Testament in which the word *ekklesia* appears in the mouth of Jesus.

> If your brother sins against you, go and tell him his fault, between you and him alone. If he listens to you, you have gained your brother. But if he does not listen, take one or two others along with you, that every charge may be established by the evidence of two or three witnesses. If he refuses to listen to them, tell it to the *ekklesia*. And if he refuses to listen even to the *ekklesia*, let him be to you as a Gentile and a tax collector (Matt 18:15–17).[20]

The members of the *ekklesia* of Christ have a responsibility to one another. They get involved in each other's business. Several years ago I attended a wedding in which the preacher challenged the wedding guests: "we are all witnesses to the vows that this couple has taken; therefore the responsibility falls on each one of us to help them keep these vows." We are all implicated. It reminds me of the teaching on baptism in the early Christian (late-first or early-second century) document called the *Didache*. According to the *Didache* 7.3, baptism was such a momentous event that the person getting baptized should fast for a few days beforehand—but not just the baptizand, but also the baptizer and other willing members of the congregation. The baptism of a new member of the community was an important event for the community, in part because of the responsibility such an additional member placed on the group, responsibility for care and discipline. Dietrich Bonhoeffer could even say:

Christians must bear the burden of one another. They must suffer and endure one another. Only as a burden is the other really a brother or sister and not just an object to be controlled.[21]

The importance of community is perhaps more apparent than ever in our fractured age. For example, some people long for association through living in shared spaces. The website for The Cohousing Association of the United States (cohousing.org) provides this definition:

Cohousing is community designed to foster connection. Physical spaces allow neighbors to easily interact with others just outside private homes. Common areas including kitchen, dining space and gardens bring people together. Collaborative decision-making builds relationships.[22]

Another example: a few years ago in his *New York Times* column, David Brooks quoted the long-time youth activist Bill Milliken as saying, "I still haven't seen one program change one kid's life. What changes people is relationships. Somebody willing to walk through the shadow of the valley of adolescence with them." Brooks added this comment on problems he sees in America: "It's a crisis of solidarity, a crisis of segmentation, spiritual degradation and intimacy."[23] What Milliken and Brooks are advocating is a version of what James Davison Hunter has called "faithful presence," which involves being "fully present" toward God and imitating God by being fully present toward each other in terms of seeking the good of others through sacrificial love.[24]

Being fully present requires full, physical presence, a

fact that reminds us of the "assembly" definition of *ekklesia*. Miliken's comments also call to mind the observer effect, the influence on phenomena caused by the mere presence of the observer, as when one measures a tire's pressure by releasing some of that pressure. The presence of people—whether in "the shadow of the valley of adolescence" or otherwise— necessarily has an effect on those around them. When I weigh the pros and cons of teaching Filipino students via Zoom versus getting on a plane and spending two weeks in country to teach them in person, I cannot properly make that evaluation without rereading a letter written to me a few years ago by a couple of those Filipinos: "Seeing you keep on coming back here just sends a great joy in our hearts." Wholly apart from the content transmitted through teaching, the teacher's physical presence has an immeasurable (literally) impact on his or her students. Three quarters of a century earlier, Bonhoeffer had exclaimed: "The physical presence of other Christians is a source of incomparable joy and strength to the believer."[25] And forty years after Bonhoeffer, Woody Allen observed that "showing up is eighty percent of success."[26] Faithful presence, showing up, walking with others—while I refrain from citing a percentage —is a great deal of what life (and certainly Christianity) is about. Even Job's friends knew that much.

Community can also be fragile and should not be taken for granted. In the book written as a reflection on his experience running a small seminary for a couple years, Bonhoeffer had much to say on Christian community.[27] He called his book *Life Together* (*Gemeinsames Leben*). His seminary at Finkenwalde gave him the chance to work out ideas already expressed in his doctoral dissertation (written at age 21), in which he asserted, "Christ ... is present only in the church

[*Kirche*], that is, where the Christian church-community [*Gemeinde*] is united by preaching and the Lord's Supper in mutual Christian love."[28] In *Life Together*, Bonhoeffer recognized that the gift of community could be taken away at any moment,[29] as it was for him when the government closed his seminary. At all times there are some Christians separated from the community by sickness, or prison, or missionary work. For Christians thus isolated, a visit is a special grace: "The prisoner, the sick person, the Christian living in the diaspora recognizes in the nearness of a fellow Christian a physical sign of the gracious presence of the triune God" (29). Would Bonhoeffer have said that the same effect could be achieved via Zoom? I think he would have recognized, as most of us do, that such technological substitutes for presence are good but not great. He knew that Christians in far away places "are strengthened by letters written by the hands of other Christians. Paul's greetings in his letters written in his own hand were no doubt tokens of such community" (30). A few years later, Bonhoeffer himself, then in Tegel prison, would receive a letter from Eberhard Bethge, in which he would read the words, "your letters, and the visit, were something of a liberation for me."[30]

Zoom is not nothing; nor is it all that God wants for us. God wants—and humans need—community. That is the meaning of the term *ekklesia*, about which we should perhaps draw one further point. Earlier we saw that "assembly" might not work as a translation for every appearance of *ekklesia* in the New Testament because, according to the Pauline letters, the word *ekklesia* can encompass the worldwide body of Christ, and the local *ekklesia* continues to exist after the assembly is concluded. But does the local *ekklesia* exist if it does not assemble at all? Scholars have pointed out an easily-missed feature of Paul's language in his two longest letters. The Christians in both Rome and Corinth typically gathered in several house churches (cf. Rom 16:5) rather than in large city-wide assemblies. But Paul makes a distinction in how he addresses the Christians of each city: he greets the "*ekklesia* of God that is in Corinth" (1 Cor 1:2), whereas Romans begins with no greeting to the "*ekklesia* in Rome." It is probable that in Paul's day the Christians in Rome never had occasion to assemble all together, whereas such an assembly did take place occasionally in Corinth. The intermittent gatherings of all the Christians in Corinth meant that Paul could address the single *ekklesia* in the city, whereas in Rome, there was no single *ekklesia* but a variety of them.[31] The *ekklesia* continues to exist after the assembly is dismissed, but if the assembly never assembles, there is no *ekklesia*, except in the broadest (worldwide) sense. The community must commune. The congregation must congregate. The church must assemble.

***

Man's chief end is to glorify God, and to enjoy him forever.
　　—Westminster Shorter Catechism (1647)

The church fails. It is probably a safe guess that the church has fallen short of its principles more than any other institution in human history. When the task is to grow into the likeness of Jesus (Eph 4:12–16), people are going to fall short of that goal, and followers of Christ have often not even made the attempt to follow Christ. The gate is narrow and the way is strait. Certainly Bonhoeffer had his own disappointments with the church, with people around him not following the path of *Discipleship*, with those who called themselves the Confessing Church not living up to their confession.[32] Maybe that is part of the reason that Bonhoeffer, who praised Christian community as a manifestation of Christ in the world, wrote to Bethge from prison: "By the way, I miss worship so remarkably little. What is the reason for this?"[33]

In the Bible, God uses various catastrophes to communicate with people—sometimes even sending plagues in order to bring about repentance (Amos 4:10). It would be irresponsible to claim that God sent any particular pandemic on a people for punishment or to compel repentance. It would be unbiblical to say that God does not do that sort of thing. It would be arrogant to say that God has no reason to do such a thing to us.

We have lived through a time in which the church in many countries, including the United States (where I live), was forbidden for a time from meeting together in large groups for worship. We might consider whether God had a hand in bringing about this result.[34] Often we look at such things along the lines of the prayer Homer Simpson once offered in response to a flood in Springfield: "Surely this has proven whatever point you had."[35] We cry out to God asking for the strangeness to end, assuring him that He has proven whatever point He had, and asking for Him to restore normalcy. Perhaps "back to normal" is not high on God's list of priorities. When Martin Luther King, Jr., gave his speech on August 28, 1963, from the steps of the Lincoln Memorial, it became known as the "I Have a Dream" speech, but one of the original titles in draft form was "Normalcy Never

Again." King was not interested in getting back to normal. Perhaps God is not either.

In Jeremiah 7, the people of Judah insisted to the prophet that normal life would continue, that God loved the status quo, that the temple in Jerusalem assured them of divine favor. Their slogan, as quoted by the prophet, was "This is the temple of YHWH, the temple of YHWH, the temple of YHWH" (Jer 7:4). Jeremiah declared that God had no love for the building that Judah had turned into "a den of robbers" (v. 11), that God, in fact, planned on knocking the building down (which he would accomplish through Nebuchadnezzar's Babylon; Jer 25:9). He cited the example of the previous Israelite shrine at Shiloh, now defunct. According to Jeremiah, it was Israel's God who caused the desolation of that shrine (vv. 12–15). God was interested in worship only from people dedicated to God's ways.

> For if you truly amend your ways and your doings, if you truly act justly one with another, if you do not oppress the alien, the orphan, and the widow, or shed innocent blood in this place, and if you do not go after other gods to your own hurt, then I will dwell with you in this place, in the land that I gave of old to your ancestors forever and ever. ... Will you steal, murder, commit adultery, swear falsely, make offerings to Baal, and go after other gods that you have not known, and then come and stand before me in this house, which is called by my name, and say, "We are safe!"—only to go on doing all these abominations? (Jer 7:5–10)

Such a declaration should cause us little surprise. It is

not the only time in Israel's Scriptures in which God specifies some prerequisites to worship, without which worship
itself is distasteful to God, or worse. Perhaps most famous is
Amos.

> I hate, I despise your festivals,
> and I take no delight in your solemn
>   assemblies.
> Even though you offer me your burnt
>   offerings,
> I will not accept them;
> and the offerings of well-being of your fatted
>   animals
> I will not look upon.
> Take away from me the noise of your songs;
> I will not listen to the melody of your harps.
> But let justice roll down like waters,
> and righteousness like an ever-flowing
>   stream.
> (Amos 5:21–24; cf. Isa 1:10–15; Mal 1:10;
>   Ps 40:6; 50:7–15; 51:16–17; 69:30–31)

Jesus finds occasion to quote twice (Matt 9:13; 12:7) the
words of Hosea 6:6: "I desire steadfast love and not sacrifice." God is the one who commanded these acts of worship,
these sacrifices and such. And he enjoys them; they provide
a sweet savour (Lev 1:9; etc.)—when they are performed by
loving hearts attuned to God's will, attentive to his Torah.
Otherwise … "I hate, I despise your festivals."

There is a perpetual temptation for people to magnify
the importance to God of their own worship, to assume that
as long as we get worship done correctly, everything else can

take a backseat. The prophets addressed this temptation in the passages quoted earlier. Hosea provides a striking example. The first five chapters of the book of Hosea contain a near constant barrage of criticism of the worship and behavior of Israel. Then the Israelites suddenly turn toward God.

> *Come, let us return to YHWH;*
> *for it is he who has torn, and he will heal us;*
> *he has struck down, and he will bind us up.*
> *After two days he will revive us;*
> *on the third day he will raise us up,*
> *that we may live before him.*
> *Let us know, let us press on to know YHWH;*
> *his appearing is as sure as the dawn;*
> *he will come to us like the showers,*
> *like the spring rains that water the earth.*
> *(Hos 6:1–3)*

These are the right words, expressing exactly what the Israelites ought to do. They assumed, and we assume, that God will be pleased. His response:

> *What shall I do with you, O Ephraim?*
> *What shall I do with you, O Judah?*
> *Your love is like a morning cloud,*
> *like the dew that goes away early.*
> *Therefore I have hewn them by the prophets,*
> *I have killed them by the words of my*
>   *mouth,*
> *and my judgment goes forth as the light.*
> *For I desire steadfast love and not sacrifice,*

> *the knowledge of God rather than burnt*
>   *offerings.*
> (Hos 6:4–6)

God does not trust these penitents. He has seen this movie before. He knows that their love is like a morning cloud. They still have not figured out that God desires steadfast love and not sacrifice. I presume that what God means is that the Israelites are feigning repentance, though perhaps they have tricked themselves into believing that they are sincere. They believe that to get God back on their side they need to light a cow on fire, make a sacrifice, say a few words, and the relationship will be restored. If they can just do worship the way God likes it, they will be able to show that God has by now proven whatever point he had. But God repeats that they can show such a thing only if they will concentrate less on worship and more on steadfast love, less on burnt offerings and more on the knowledge of God.

The Parable of the Good Samaritan (Luke 10:30–35) reflects, in part, similar concerns. After all, Jesus chose as his examples of wrong behavior two professional worship leaders: a priest and a Levite. As they passed by the dying man on the roadside, they may have been on their way to the temple, as many readers have guessed. No matter how precise or flamboyant was the worship that they then performed, they could not be the heroes of this story, a story that illustrates once again the truth of Hosea 6:6.

Why is this a hard lesson for people to learn? Probably because worship is easy—or, at least, worship is easy when the intention behind the worship is to perform the right actions, rather than, say, to encounter God and experience transformation. It is hard to dissent from Hunter's description of the Christian task: "Only by being fully present to God as a worshipping community and as adoring followers can we be faithfully present in the world."[36] Worship may be the beginning (formation) and end (enjoyment) of the Christian life, and "man's chief end," but corporate worship is not the whole of the Christian life. In fact, worship is valuable and pleasing to God only when it serves as spiritual formation—molding worshippers into the image of Christ to then represent God in the world[37]—or as a longed-for encounter with God. All too often, worship is neither, but instead "attending worship" is the easiest way of telling others (including pollsters) and oneself that one is a Christian. For some first-century Jews, tithing may have functioned similarly. In Matthew 23:23, Jesus criticizes people who tithe garden spices to the neglect of the weightier matters of Torah. We understand the temptation: tithing spices is a lot easier than living according to justice, mercy, and faithfulness. But the Bible assures us that there are things God considers more fundamental than our worship, that he sometimes puts a stop to his people's worship when he determines that they desire a normal life rather than a faithful life. In the New Testament, Jesus instructed his disciples that there were reasons why someone might need to stop worshiping in order to take care of another priority (Matt 5:23–24). What were those reasons? Reconciliation with a brother.

If we are trying to understand how God was involved in the pandemic, why the church would face government pressure to stop worshiping corporately for a time, the Bible suggests to us that it might be time for God's people to examine whether God considers their worship a pleasing aroma. The summer of 2020—when the pandemic was still fresh and government-imposed lockdowns were still common in America, and people marched in the street demanding justice—demonstrates the continuing urgency of Jesus's advice in Matthew 5: reconciliation with one's brother should precede worship.

I am reminded of the Appendix to the first autobiography written by Frederick Douglass. In the course of the narrative of his life, Douglass had many times criticized the religion practiced by the slave holding class of the American South, a religion called Christianity. In one section, Douglass' owner "experienced religion," and thereby became even more vicious than formerly, for "after his conversion, he found religious sanction and support for his slaveholding cruelty."[38] Such passages in his narrative gave Douglass pause upon a subsequent reading, inspiring him to clarify his religious views in an appendix.

> What I have said respecting and against religion, I mean strictly to apply to the *slaveholding religion* of this land, and with no possible reference to Christianity proper; for, between the Christianity of this land, and the Christianity of Christ, I recognize the widest possible difference—so wide, that to receive the one as good, pure, and holy, is of necessity to reject the other as bad, corrupt, and wicked.[39]

This passage, which will provoke only sympathy in a twenty-first century American audience, should also remind us of the delusion that self-professing Christians can experience, in mistaking God's priorities, in valuing sacrifice and burnt offerings over steadfast love and the knowledge of God.

The recent cultural passion for reconciliation and relationships in some ways coheres with essential ideals of the church. The apostle Paul often dealt with tense situations in the communities he formed or was counseling, and he constantly advised his readers to "regard others as better than yourselves" (Phil 2:3), to "bear one another's burdens" (Gal 6:2), to consider themselves parts of the same body (1 Cor 12). This advice applied not only to people of different socio-economic backgrounds (e.g., see the comments on the Lord's Supper in 1 Cor 11) but also to people of different ethnicities (Eph 2). We find a model for such reconciliation among the original disciples of Christ, chosen by Jesus himself, a group that included both Simon the Zealot (Luke 6:15) and Matthew/Levi the tax collector (Luke 6:15; cf. 5:27)—the one an avowed enemy of Rome, the other Rome's employee.[40] (It would be nice to know how Jesus introduced them to each other, and what their reaction was.) James K. A. Smith admits that "I often tell my children that one of the reasons we go to church is to learn to love people we don't really like that much."[41] Reflecting such ideals, Hunter describes the church as community:

> It is here where we learn forgiveness and humility, practice kindness, hospitality, and charity, grow in patience and wisdom, and become clothed in compassion, gentleness, and joy. This is the crucible within which Christian holiness is forged. This is the context within which shalom is enacted.[42]

In times such as these (that is, at all times), we need to be reminded of first principles. In two passages of Matthew's Gospel, Jesus presented pictures of judgment in which people were surprised at their fate. In Matthew 7:21–23, people who had performed quite amazing works in the name of Jesus were rejected by him because they failed to do the will of the heavenly Father, i.e., all the things Jesus had talked about in the previous three chapters, including the crucial summary statement for the entire Law and Prophets: "do unto others as you would have them do unto you" (7:12). In Matthew 25:31–46, when people were separated as sheep and goats are separated by a shepherd, they were again surprised to hear their judgment, and again the criterion for judgment revolved around treatment of others. In fact, the goats here were not accused of being unusually bad: they did not steal food from the hungry, they simply did not supply the hungry with food. The goats were normal people, and they were rejected. The scene is reminiscent of Matthew 22:34–40, where we learn that Jesus's nominations for the two most important commandments are love of God and love of neighbor. I do wish we had a longer list from Jesus; I would love to know what he considered the third greatest commandment, and the fourth, and so on. But I will admit that these top two are so difficult to accomplish, and so rarely attempted, that we would do well not to allow ourselves such distractions.

Is it possible that the pandemic could be good for the church? Not if we insist on a return to normalcy, assuring God that he has proven whatever point he had. God may want to shout at us, "normalcy never again!" But if we use this season as an opportunity to reflect on the extent to which our priorities align with those of the God whom we worship, to remember that corporate worship is important to God and to us and that certain behaviors and attitudes serve as essential prerequisites to worship, we might find that God can use this pandemic to bring us closer to him.

***

The church is, first and foremost, a worshipping community whose life centers on the word of God.

   —James Davison Hunter[43]

A worshipping community. I think most Christians I know would readily identify worship as something essential to the church. A community? I'm not so sure, even though that's what the very term *ekklesia* means. More—a community of people with responsibilities to one another, who must become burdens to each other, who must be fully present to one another in order to be fully present to God (and vice versa), who must model among themselves the reconciliation and relationships to which God calls all people. One of the lessons the pandemic ought to teach the church is that God's *ekklesia* should endeavor more intentionally to be the community imagined by Jesus so that this community can worship God in a way he finds more pleasing.

Endnotes

[1] This essay was written in the summer of 2021. While it perhaps retains some value outside of that context, some of its expressions apply most immediately to the early and middle pandemic. This chapter first appeared in *Journal of Christian Studies* 1 (2022): 9–25.

   [2] I do not mean that avoiding people was a character trait of the priest and Levite, but that in this instance (in the parable) they did so. To avoid unduly negative interpretations of this priest and Levite, see Amy-Jill Levin, *Short Stories by*

Jesus: The Enigmatic Parables of a Controversial Rabbi (New York: HarperOne, 2014), 90–95.

[3] Mark A. Yarhouse, *Understanding Gender Dysphoria: Navigating Transgender Issues in a Changing Culture* (Downers Grove, IL: IVP, 2015), 37.

[4] C. S. Lewis, *The Four Loves* (London: Geoffrey Bles, 1960), 10.

[5] Paul Trebilco, *Self-designations and Group Identity in the New Testament* (Cambridge: Cambridge University Press, 2012), 16; John M. G. Barclay, "An Identity Received from God: The Theological Configuration of Paul's Kinship Discourse," *Early Christianity* 8 (2017): 354–72.

[6] Matthew V. Novenson points out that Paul's habit of naming people in his letters with a single name—something similar to a modern American using someone's first name rather than first and last names—"reinforces the corporate perception of kinship among the Pauline believers"; *Christ among the Messiahs: Christ Language in Paul and Messiah Language in Ancient Judaism* (Oxford: Oxford University Press, 2012), 83, within a discussion of ancient naming practices, pp. 72–84.

[7] C. K. Barrett, *Church, Ministry, and Sacraments in the New Testament* (Grand Rapids: Eerdmans, 1985), 9.

[8] The English word "church" derives through German (where the word is *Kirche*) ultimately from Greek κυριακόν ("lordly"), an adjective cognate to κύριος ("lord"), a frequent New Testament title for Jesus. The adjective itself appears twice in the New Testament (1 Cor 11:20; Rev 1:10). In the fourth century, κυριακόν could refer to a church building (e.g., Eusebius, *Ecclesiastical History* 9.10.12). When Christians today use the word "church" to refer to the church building, they unwittingly echo the

fourth-century usage of this Greek word. But, of course, the word "church" in the English Bible, as a translation of ἐκκλησία, encompasses the people and not the building.

⁹ The KJV uses "church" at Acts 7:38, but more recent translations have "congregation" (ESV, NRSV).

¹⁰ See David Daniell, *William Tyndale: A Biography* (New Haven, CT: Yale University Press, 1994), 122, 148.

¹¹ Frederick William Danker, ed., *A Greek-English Lexicon of the New Testament and Other Early Christian Literature*, 3d ed. (Chicago: University of Chicago Press, 2000), 303–4.

¹² For an argument in this regard, see Trebilco, *Self-designations*, 188–90.

¹³ See the brief entry on *ekklesia* in *The Cambridge Greek Lexicon* (Cambridge: Cambridge University Press, 2021), 447. The first definition is quoted above, for which the recommended gloss is "assembly"; the second definition offers the glosses "congregation or church." The *Brill Dictionary of Ancient Greek* (Leiden: Brill, 2014), 632, has a longer entry with more detailed references, but the result is essentially the same. The first definition is: "assembly of people called together." The end of the entry provides a definition for the LXX ("community") and for the New Testament ("Church, community of the Christians").

¹⁴ T. Muraoka, *A Greek-English Lexicon of the Septuagint* (Leuven: Peeters, 2009), 209: (1) "act of congregating"; (2) "large group of gathered people"; (3) "a social organisation and body."

¹⁵ For references to Philo, see Trebilco, *Self-designations*, 165–69.

¹⁶ Andrie Du Toit, "Paulus Oecumenicus: Interculturality in the Shaping of Paul's Theology," *New Testament*

Studies 55 (2009): 121–43, at 133–34. For discussion, see also Trebilco, *Self-designations*, 169–80. For example, Colossians uses *ekklesia* for a local group (Col 4:15, 16) but also for "the universal church" (Col 1:18, 24). In Ephesians, all nine appearances of *ekklesia* (1:22; 3:10, 21; 5:23–32) refer to the universal church (Trebilco, 198–99). This usage of *ekklesia* for a non-local entity is the one situation in which BDAG suggests translating "church" (definition 3c); also Trebilco (165n6), who explains that "assembly" cannot accommodate a "universal" meaning in English. In such cases, Tyndale still used "congregation."

[17] This example is given by Moisés Silva, *Biblical Words and Their Meaning: An Introduction to Lexical Semantics*, 2d ed. (Grand Rapids: Zondervan, 1994), 45, 48.

[18] See also John 15:19; 17:13–19. On some of the difficulties of Christian disentanglement from the world, see James Davison Hunter, *To Change the World: The Irony, Tragedy, and Possibility of Christianity in the Late Modern World* (Oxford: Oxford University Press, 2010), 176–93.

[19] On Paul's ecclesiocentric interpretation, see especially Richard B. Hays, *Echoes of Scripture in the Letters of Paul* (New Haven, CT: Yale University Press, 1989).

[20] ESV, altered by replacing "church" with *ekklesia*.

[21] Dietrich Bonhoeffer, *Life Together* (1940), trans. Geffrey B. Kelly, Dietrich Bonhoeffer Works 5 (Minneapolis: Fortress, 1996), 100. Here Bonhoeffer is reflecting on Galatians 6:2.

[22] See Liuan Huska, "Cohousing: The New American Family," *Christianity Today* (28 Nov. 2016), https://www.christianitytoday.com/ct/2016/november-web-only/cohousing-new-american-family.html.

[23] David Brooks, "The Power of a Dinner Table," *The*

New York Times (18 Oct. 2016). On Bill Milliken, see https://www.communitiesinschools.org/about-us/our-leadership/profile/william-milliken.

[24] Hunter, *To Change the World*, 238–86. See the succinct discussion on pp. 243–48.

[25] Bonhoeffer, *Life Together*, 29.

[26] On the sources of this quotation and its variant with "life" instead of "success," see https://quoteinvestigator.com/2013/06/10/showing-up/.

[27] For a recent treatment of the Finkenwalde seminary, see Charles Marsh, *Strange Glory: A Life of Dietrich Bonhoeffer* (New York: Knopf, 2014), 231–32.

[28] This is part of the dissertation (completed in 1927) that was omitted from the form originally published in 1930, but it is included in the notes of the now-standard English edition: Dietrich Bonhoeffer, *Sanctorum Communio: A Theological Study of the Sociology of the Church*, trans. Reinhard Krauss and Nancy Lukens, ed. Clifford J. Green, Dietrich Bonhoeffer Works 1 (Minneapolis: Fortress, 1998), 138. See also Green's discussion of this passage at pp. 15–16.

[29] Bonhoeffer, *Life Together*, 30.

[30] Letter from Eberhard Bethge to Dietrich Bonhoeffer, 2 Jan. 1944, in *Letters and Papers from Prison*, ed. John W. De Gruchy, Dietrich Bonhoeffer Works 8 (Minneapolis: Fortress, 2010), 248, document #94. The theme of letters substituting for physical presence is common. See Jerome, *Epistle* 7.2, writing from isolation in the desert of Chalcis during the 370s AD: "Now I speak with your letter, I embrace it, it converses with me, for it is the only thing here that knows Latin. For here it is necessary either to speak a language barbarous for an old man or to remain silent. And as often as the impressed tracks of the well-familiar hand

recalls the faces dear to me, so often either I am no longer here or you are here."

[31] See Trebilco, *Self-designations*, 171.

[32] See Victoria Barnett, *For the Soul of My People: Protestant Protest against Hitler* (Oxford: Oxford University Press, 1992).

[33] Letter from Dietrich Bonhoeffer to Eberhard Bethge, 15 Dec. 1943, in *Letters and Papers from Prison*, 223 (document #86).

[34] The fictional Reverend John Ames almost preached a sermon on the divine intention behind the 1918 Spanish Flu; reflecting back on the incident, he wrote: "I believe that plague was a great sign to us, and we refused to see it and take its meaning, and since then we have had war continuously." Marilynne Robinson, *Gilead* (New York: Farrar, Straus and Giroux, 2004), 43.

[35] The prayer comes near the end of the episode "Pray Anything," season 14, episode 10, of *The Simpsons* (original air date: 9 Feb. 2003).

[36] Hunter, *To Change the World*, 244.

[37] On such a view of worship, see the previous essay; and James K. A. Smith, *Desiring the Kingdom: Worship, Worldview, and Cultural Formation* (Grand Rapids: Baker, 2009).

[38] Frederick Douglass, *Narrative of the Life of Frederick Douglass, an American Slave* (1845), ch. 10. I have used the edition in *The Portable Frederick Douglass*, ed. John Stauffer and Henry Louis Gates, Jr. (New York: Penguin, 2016), 51.

[39] Douglass, *Narrative*, 94.

[40] I am assuming the traditional interpretation identifying Matthew with Levi, in accordance with the Gospel of Matthew, which tells the story of Levi the tax collector (Mark 2:13–17; Luke 5:27–32) under the name of Matthew

(Matthew 9:9–13). Describing a tax (or toll) collector as "Rome's employee" is a bit overstated; see David J. Downs, "Economics," in *Dictionary of Jesus and the Gospels*, 2d ed., ed. Joel B. Green (Downers Grove, IL: IVP, 2013), 219–26. Still, the point stands: a Jewish zealot and a Jewish tax collector would have made odd roommates.

[41] Smith, *Desiring the Kingdom*, 202.

[42] Hunter, *To Change the World*, 253.

[43] Hunter, *To Change the World*, 184.

Section 4
Miscellaneous

Chapter 19

What Is a Canon?[1]

The biblical canon is an idea, a concept that exists inside someone's head. When biblical scholars use the term "canon," they refer to the collection of Scriptures that Jews or Christians consider to have binding authority. Today there is not just one canon, but multiple; different Christian groups sometimes have different biblical canons. These differences are sometimes reflected in the physical Bibles they use, but, as we shall see, not always. As I said, the biblical canon—the identity of the authoritative books—is really an idea in someone's head. That fact makes it a little difficult to interpret correctly the contents of someone's biblical canon—certainly, an ancient someone's biblical canon—even when they list its contents for us. Nevertheless, despite the difficulties of interpreting biblical canon lists, they do provide our surest guide to what an ancient person considered canonical.

In this essay, I want to discuss some of the difficulties in interpreting the biblical canon lists that have been preserved for us from Late Antiquity. But first I want to clarify why I think the canon lists are important by explaining why other possible (and frequently cited) sources of information for the biblical canon can be misleading in that regard.

My contention is that we are on the safest ground in determining which books ancient people considered canonical when they explicitly tell us which books they considered canonical.

Manuscripts: Canon as a Physical Object?

Scholars studying the biblical canon have routinely discussed biblical manuscripts as important sources— whether we're talking about the Dead Sea Scrolls or the Greek biblical pandects from the fourth century CE (Vaticanus, Sinaiticus). I don't dispute that these manuscripts do provide important information regarding the canon (which I will discuss later), but the basic methodological problem I want to highlight here is that manuscripts are not canon lists.

The general idea is clear for modern Bibles. In the twenty-first century, people own Bibles that contain more than what they consider canonical, and they know which parts count as canonical because they've got a concept of canon in their heads. No one I know considers the maps in their Bibles to be canonical, or the cross-references or the introductions or essays or notes. Some people own Bibles with apocrypha despite their strong adherence to the Protestant biblical canon; they would tell you that not everything in their Bible is canonical. But if you picked up their Bible, you wouldn't be able to tell which parts they consider noncanonical.

So it has always been.

Hugh of Saint Victor in the twelfth century said that not

everything "in the Old Testament" is "included in the canon," such as the Wisdom of Solomon (*in Veteri Testamento, ut diximus, quidam libri sunt qui non scribuntur in canone*).[2] A few centuries later, the Scandinavian Lutheran Niels Hemmingsen (1555) averred that (in the summary of John H. Hayes) "writings could be found in the Bible but not be canonical (authoritative)."[3] The same sort of idea is expressed in the anti-Catholic Russian Orthodox Archbishop Feofan Prokopovich (1681–1726):

> There is no doubt that not all the books contained in this volume that is called the Bible are canonical. There are some in it which are not guaranteed by any divine testimony, which are not canonical, and which are given the name Apocrypha.[4]

I grant that these three examples—the only examples I can cite right now who are so explicit about the point I want to make—all come from people who could be considered somewhat unusual with regard to the biblical canon that they advocate. Modern scholars might object that these three authors from the second millennium do not have much in common with early Christians in their views on the biblical canon.

What about Athanasius? The fourth-century bishop of Alexandria produced what is probably the most famous canon list today, since it provides the earliest preserved list of books for the New Testament that matches the now-dominant 27-book New Testament (*Festal Letter* 39).[5] As for the Old Testament, Athanasius more-or-less stood with every other Greek canon list we have from the fourth century in limiting his Old Testament to the twenty-two books of the

Jews,[6] though Athanasius did exclude Esther from the canon. According to Athanasius, such canonical books are

> the springs of salvation, so that someone who thirsts may be satisfied by the words they contain. In these books alone the teaching of piety is proclaimed. Let no one add or subtract anything from them. (§19)[7]

But Athanasius did not think that these canonical books were the only writings a Christian should read. He continues:

> But for the sake of greater accuracy, I add this, writing from necessity. There are other books, outside of the preceding, which have not be canonized, but have been prescribed by the ancestors to be read to those who newly join us and want to be instructed in the word of piety: the Wisdom of Solomon, the Wisdom of Sirach, Esther, Judith, Tobit, the book called Teaching of the Apostles, and the Shepherd. Nevertheless, beloved, the former books are canonized; the latter are (only) read; and there is no mention of the apocryphal books. (§§ 20–21)

Athanasius discusses three categories of books here: (1) the canonized books; (2) the books that are not canonized but still read by Christians, especially those new to the faith; and (3) apocrypha. Obviously Athanasius does not define the word "apocrypha" the same way as Protestants do; Athanasius means books like *1 Enoch* or the *Gospel of Thomas*, and these are books that Athanasius thinks would not be valuable to a Christian.

The middle category of books—the valuable but not

canonized books—include some of the books Protestants consider the Old Testament Apocrypha (but not Maccabees), one book included in the Jewish Bible (Esther), and a couple of books included in the Apostolic Fathers (as the books in that modern collection have been known for a few centuries now).[8]

Now, to go back to manuscripts. It has often been pointed out that the Old Testament of Codex Vaticanus corresponds precisely with the Old Testament books included in Athanasius' first two categories. As for the New Testament, we can't be sure, because Vaticanus breaks off in Hebrews, so which books appeared after that must remain in some ways a mystery. Now, a question about which we can only take educated guesses: would Athanasius have objected to Codex Vaticanus containing Wisdom of Solomon? Or Esther? Or Tobit? After all, Athanasius insisted that these books were not a part of the biblical canon. Then again, he also insisted that these same books were useful to Christians. The latter sentiment leads me to assume Athanasius would not have objected to a biblical manuscript that included these non-canonical books, but may have even desired it.

And that means that the contents of such a biblical manuscript would not have corresponded to Athanasius' biblical canon. Or, to echo the words of Feofan Prokopovich, not all the books in the Bible are in the canon.

Canon is a concept, an idea. If we equate the Bible with the canon, then the Bible is also a concept. But often we define the Bible as a physical object, in which case the Bible is not the canon. The biblical canon is not a physical object.

Quotations: Canon through Citation?

Ancient Jews and Christians quoted the Bible a lot, and these quotations provide extremely helpful information regarding the development of the biblical canon. But lists of quoted books, even lists of books quoted *as scripture*, are not the same as canon lists.

Once again, Athanasius provides a good example. Remember that Athanasius did not consider Wisdom of Solomon to be canonized, and yet he cites the work several times in his writings, three times under the title *graphē* (*C. Gent.* 11; 17; *C. Ar.* 2.79).[9] He treats the Shepherd of Hermas similarly; in one passage (*Decr.* 18.3), he quotes Herm. Mand. 1.1 (26.1) with this introduction: "and in the Shepherd it is written (γέγραπται), since they [= the Eusebians] bring forward even this book, though it is not in the canon." This passage (*Decr.* 18.3) is the very one that scholars often point to as providing the earliest attestation of the word *kanōn* used in reference to the biblical canon.[10] Athanasius excludes the Shepherd from the canon, and then quotes it with the introductory term γέγραπται.

The list of writings quoted by Athanasius is not equivalent to Athanasius' canon. The list of writings quoted "as Scripture" by Athanasius is not equivalent to Athanasius' canon. We might consider this idea non-sensical: what could be the difference between Scripture and canon? But scholars have distinguished the two concepts for decades now, and Athanasius did, too (though in a different way). The canonized books are "the springs of salvation ... [wherein] alone the teaching of piety is proclaimed." Their number is subject to neither addition or subtraction (*Ep. fest.* 39.19; quoted above). The books in the middle category (not canonized but read) have been traditionally assigned (according to Athanasius) for elementary instruction "in the word of piety" (§20).

I interpret these sentiments in harmony with other patristic evidence to mean that a faithful Christian should never disagree with a canonized book (it is absolutely authoritative), though some other books are very helpful for understanding aspects of the faith—they provide good, basic introductions to Christian theology and morality—but their authority is not absolute (there might be occasion to set them aside).[11] Maybe we can think about Athanasius' view of Wisdom of Solomon and the Shepherd of Hermas as something like the reception of *Mere Christianity* among many modern Christians.[12]

Some Problems with Canon Lists

I have argued that the canon lists provide our primary point of entry into thinking about which writings ancient Christians considered canonical. That is not to say that the interpretation of the canon lists entails no problems. I end this essay with reflections on just two of these difficulties.

(1) The representative nature of the canon lists.

It is safest to say that a particular author's canon list represents the canon of that particular author. There were disagreements on the precise limits of the biblical canon in antiquity. (Such disagreements have never ended.) The canon lists themselves are products of these disagreements; there would have been less need to produce such lists if there were universal agreement on what should be included. No patristic author had the authority to end all discussion on the matter. The Christian biblical canon was not definitively settled in the fourth century.

Let me say, however, that there is an impressively consistent core of books across the spectrum of canon lists. In the fourth century, among Christians both Arian and pro-Nicene and everywhere in between, arguments did not hinge on which books someone accepted as canonical. Everyone accepted the Pentateuch as canonical, and the Four Gospels, and the letters of Paul (with some uncertainty about Hebrews), and much else. Just because the canon was not definitively settled across the board—people could still disagree about the status of Tobit—does not mean people were flying completely blind. Nobody disputed that Isaiah was God's word; nobody would have been willing to respond to an Isaian prooftext from their theological opponent by saying that Isaiah's words were irrelevant.

There has been a long-standing scholarly dispute about the best way to define "canon": whether as a list of authoritative books or as an authoritative list of books (to echo Metzger).[13] A similar distinction is sometimes labeled "Canon 1" (= open canon) and "Canon 2" (= closed canon).

However helpful these distinctions may be, I'm not all that interested in them. When it comes to the canon lists, we would of course recognize that these lists represent "Canon 2"; they are authoritative lists of books—but, only for the specific author drafting the list, and whoever happens to grant to that author authority sufficient to determine their own canon. Athanasius did not settle the canon for the whole church. His canon list represents the canon of Athanasius and those within his jurisdiction. Same for Augustine, Jerome, and even Pope Innocent I.

And even limiting the authority of the canon list to its own author, we're not out of trouble. We've already seen that Athanasius grants some version of authority to works outside his list of canonized books. He's not the only one to do this.[14] When in a single passage Athanasius denies canonical authority to a writing and cites that same writing authoritatively, the good bishop has presented us with an intriguing notion of authority that transcends (or combines?) the usual distinctions between Canon 1 and Canon 2.

(2) The words on the page.

Sometimes the very words constituting a canon list are difficult to interpret. If we're looking at a Christian canon list, we have a pretty good idea of what they meant by "Genesis" or "Isaiah" or "Luke." But especially for certain Old Testament books, there is some ambiguity. This applies particularly to Esther, Daniel, Jeremiah, and Ezra, each of which exists in multiple versions, versions that differ quite substantially.

Here is one instance in this discussion where biblical manuscripts prove very helpful—essential, really. When a canon list mentions "Daniel," we should almost always assume that this title referred (in the mind of the composer of the canon list) to the long version of Daniel, inclusive of the deuterocanonical additions (Susanna, Bel & the Dragon, and the Prayer of Azariah and the Hymn of the Three Young Men). We can make this assumption because the version of Daniel known from the Christian manuscripts is this long form.

This example raises questions, such as: to what extent would a patristic author (or someone today) have thought that a particular textual form of a book was canonical? That's a difficult question; in regard to the additions to Daniel, sometimes these additions appear separately within canon lists (i.e., Susanna listed as a separate item), so we can say that at least some people thought of these texts as perhaps not integral to Daniel and yet still canonical.

And then there's Jerome's Latin version of Daniel. Jerome translated from a Hebrew/Aramaic text that included none of the deuterocanonical additions. He translated these additions from Theodotion's Greek text and prefixed an obelus (resembling a hyphen or dash) to their every line. In the preface to his translation he explains that these additions are not found in the Hebrew text, and that the obelus is intended to "slay" them. When readers encountered this version of Daniel, with the additions preceded by obelus, what did they think? Were the additions canonical? Latin manuscripts often do not transmit the obeli, such as the Codex Amiatinus from around 700, or Theodulf's Bibles from the next century, but these Bibles do preserve Jerome's notes explaining the absence of the additions from the Hebrew Bible.

When a canon list simply says "Daniel," we are still left with questions about how the author of the list thought about the alternative versions transmitted under this one title.

Conclusion

The development of the Bible has attracted a great deal of scholarly and popular attention because it is a fascinating subject with vexing problems and surprising twists. The canon lists are an essential part of such study. Though at times difficult to interpret, they provide essential information on how ancient Christians parsed the status of the various religious books available to them.

Endnotes

[1] First appeared at the *Bible and Interpretation* website (August 2019), https://bibleinterp.arizona.edu/articles/what-canon.

[2] The Latin is in Migne, PL 175.16a. The translation is from Frans Van Liere, trans., "Hugh of Saint Victor: *On Sacred Scripture and Its Authors; The Diligent Examiner*," in *Interpretation of Scripture: Theory. A Selection of Works of Hugh, Andrew, Richard and Godfrey of St Victor, and of Robert Melun*, ed. Franklin T. Harkins and Frans van Liere (Turnhout: Brepols, 2012), 203–52, at 219.

[3] John H. Hayes, "Historical Criticism of the Old Testament Canon," in *Hebrew Bible / Old Testament: The History of Its Interpretation*, ed. Magne Sæbø, vol. 2: *From the Renaissance to the Enlightenment* (Göttingen: Vandenhoeck & Ruprecht, 2008), 985–1005, at 990.

[4] Quoted in Ephrem Lash, "The Canon of Scripture in the Orthodox Church," in *The Canon of Scripture in Jewish and Christian Tradition*, ed. Philip S. Alexander and Jean-Daniel Kaestli (Prahins: Éditions du Zèbre, 2007), 217–32, at 228.

[5] Edmon L. Gallagher and John D. Meade, *The Biblical Canon Lists from Early Christianity: Texts and Analysis* (Oxford: Oxford University Press, 2017), 118–29.

[6] See the other lists in Gallagher and Meade, *Biblical Canon Lists*, ch. 3.

[7] Text and translation from Gallagher and Meade, *Biblical Canon Lists*, 124. The translation is adapted from David Brakke, "A New Fragment of Athanasius' Thirty-Ninth *Festal Letter*: Heresy, Apocrypha, and the Canon," *Harvard Theological Review* 103 (2010): 47–66. See now

the comprehensive translation of Athanasius' festal letters in *The Festal Letters of Athanasius of Alexandria, with the Festal Index and the Historia Acephala*, trans. and comm. David Brakke and David M. Gwynn (Liverpool: Liverpool University Press, 2022).

[8] See David Lincicum, "The Paratextual Invention of the Term 'Apostolic Fathers'," *Journal of Theological Studies* 66 (2015): 139–48.

[9] See J. Leemans, "Athanasius and the Book of Wisdom," *Ephemerides Theologicae Lovanienses* 73 (1997): 349–68.

[10] Bruce M. Metzger, *The Canon of the New Testament: Its Origin, Development, and Significance* (Oxford: Oxford University Press, 1987), 292.

[11] See further Edmon L. Gallagher, "Origen on the Shepherd of Hermas," *Early Christianity* 10 (2019): 201–15.

[12] See George M. Marsden, *C. S. Lewis's Mere Christianity: A Biography* (Princeton: Princeton University Press, 2016).

[13] Metzger, *Canon of the New Testament*, 282.

[14] See again Gallagher, "Origen on the Shepherd of Hermas."

Chapter 20

My Friend Doesn't Believe in God

An Address to Teenagers[1]

L iving in the buckle of the Bible Belt, I don't know a whole lot of people who would deny the existence of God, though there are plenty of people—and there always have been—who act like atheists. In America, including the South, atheism is more common than ever, and even if we don't know any full-blown atheists, the chances are pretty good that we know people (a bunch of people) who simply don't care about God or religion. You probably go to church with some of them.

I have known and do know a few atheists in my time. About a decade ago I took some mission trips to Albania in Europe, which is a country that was communist and explicitly anti-religious for about fifty years in the twentieth century, so there are a lot of people there who don't go to church (or the mosque—many lapsed Muslims there) because they grew up not caring and not believing. Right now in my hometown, I know some students from China, who—as you would expect—know almost nothing about

Christianity or any other religion. An old college friend of mine, an American, a Tennessean, who grew up going to church and went to college to become a minister eventually decided that, even though he appreciates the church very much, he simply does not have faith in God. And of course there are those atheists (none of whom I know personally) who are very opposed to religion as something only idiots would accept. There are all kinds of reasons that someone might not believe in God. Each story is different.

What can we do? You are probably going to school with some people who don't believe in God. You may be close friends with some of them. You can do several things to be a positive influence on those people.

#1 Don't be a hypocrite. You know what a hypocrite is, right? Someone who says one thing and does another. Someone who doesn't practice what he or she preaches. In our case, it would be someone who talks about religion and doesn't live out his or her religion. Someone who professes a belief in God but doesn't act like it. People who don't go to church consistently say that one major reason they dislike religion is because of hypocrites—the people at church telling them how to live their life, what sins to avoid, and then those same people go out and practice those very sins. The people telling them that they shouldn't drink alcohol go get drunk at a party on Friday night. The people telling them they shouldn't have sex either go as far with their boyfriends/girlfriends as they can without actually having sex, or even they are more promiscuous than the kids who don't go to church. You get the point. People who end up leaving church in their 20s after having grown up Christian also consistently cite hypocrisy as one of the top reasons they just don't care anymore. If you want to help your friend, don't be a hypocrite. Practice what you preach. Be a good example of what the Christian life ought to look like.

#2 Be quiet. Just shut up. There are too many people talking these days, under the impression that the world needs to hear everything that pops into their heads. And they have plenty of (online) outlets to tell the world their every thought, especially when they think someone else is wrong. They want to make it clear, in no uncertain terms, that this other person is not only wrong but a fool. If you want to be a positive influence on people, do not engage in this nonsense. Behave in the way that the apostle Paul advised the Thessalonians to live (1 Thess 4:11–12). Think about how Peter told wives to influence their godless husbands (1 Pet 3:4).

What I'm telling you is do not get into arguments (whether online or in person) with your friends who don't believe in God. When you get into an argument, you're goal is usually not to persuade the other person but to win the argument, which means making the other person look stupid. At least nine times out of ten, either you're going to be the one who looks stupid, or if you do "win the argument," you're going to look mean and hateful. This is not helpful. So be quiet. Listen. Respond with grace when someone asks you something, and avoid arguments.

#3 Be ready. Peter tells his readers to "be ready at any time to give an answer to anyone who asks you for a reason for the hope that is in you" (1 Pet 3:15). Notice that Peter is not requiring people to have the answer to every possible objection. He does not mean that we need to learn about dinosaurs and how they could fit on Noah's ark, or why geologists are right or wrong about the age of the earth. But what

Peter is saying is that we need to be ready to answer people when they ask us about the hope that we have. Peter imagines that people might ask us sometime why we do what we do: why do you go to church? why do you read your Bible? why do you believe in God? We need to be ready with answers, better ones than just, "I don't know, I've never really thought about it. It's what I've always done." I'll briefly give you my answer: Christianity helps me make sense of this life, and it provides me hope in this hopeless world. I think that's something that people who don't believe in God are missing. If we're ready with compelling answers about our own faith—again, not answers to every possible objection—we might be able to help people see the value of religion and the truth of Christianity.

#4 Be comfortable and confident with your own faith. Don't be scared that someone might see things differently from you, might think you're wrong. Don't take it as a personal attack. (This will also help you avoid arguments.) Recognize—and acknowledge to your friend—that there are some legitimate questions about the nature of reality and about life and about God for which you have not (yet?) found satisfying solutions. Also recognize that these sorts of questions will always follow us, no matter what sort of religious (or non-religious) belief system we embrace. So it's no knock on Christianity that it doesn't allow us to understand every aspect of life. You didn't come to faith because you finally solved all the problems or answered every question. There was some other reason (or reasons), and I imagine that, like me, you came to faith primarily because your faith helps you to understand what this life is all about in a way far superior to what other belief systems have to offer. So, be comfortable and confident in that faith.

How do you do that? How do you become comfortable and confident in your faith? It's no big secret. You practice the spiritual disciplines, which include, at least, praying, studying Scripture, worshiping, and having spiritual conversations with spiritual people, particularly people who are more spiritually mature than you. Such practices almost always lead to stronger faith. That, in turn, allows you to engage unbelievers in conversations without feeling like your own faith is threatened by their unbelief.

Let me end with two further points, a warning and an exhortation. First, the warning. If your faith is not strong—if you don't know much Scripture or you don't pray very often —you should be wary of the influence of someone who doesn't believe in God, for the same reason that we make teenage drivers have a drivers permit for some length of time before we turn them loose on the roads. Someone with weak faith is not well-prepared to influence positively someone with no faith. The person without faith is just as likely to influence the weak believer.

Now, the exhortation. Because of your age, you are well-positioned to have a strong influence on your high school friends. Your high school friends have not become the people that they will be later in life. They are still forming; they are very susceptible to positive (and negative) influences. There is little reason to think that an unbeliever at age 15 will still be an unbeliever at age 35. (On the other hand, once you hit about 30, you're pretty much the person you're going to be. It's much harder to influence 30-year-olds to change the way they see the world.) That means that while your friends are still forming their belief systems, God may well have put you in their lives to be a positive influence on them. You could be the difference in that person's life, the influence that he or she reflects back on as first igniting the faith that he or she later cherishes.

It's your moment. Live in your faith.

Endnotes

[1] This chapter was prepared for the youth rally Evangelism University in Savannah, TN, January, 2019.

Bibliography

Allen, C. Leonard. *Distant Voices: Discovering a Forgotten Past for a Changing Church.*Abilene: ACU Press, 1993.

Augustine, *Confessions*, Translated by Thomas Williams. Indianapolis: Hackett, 2019.

Barclay, John M. G. "An Identity Received from God: The Theological Configuration of Paul's Kinship Discourse." *Early Christianity* 8 (2017): 354–72.

———. "Mirror-Reading a Polemical Letter: Galatians as a Test Case." *Journal for the Study of the New Testament* 31 (1987): 73–93.

———. "Paul, Philemon and the Dilemma of Christian Slave-Ownership." *New Testament Studies* 37 (1991): 161–86.

Barnett, Victoria. *For the Soul of My People: Protestant Protest against Hitler.* Oxford: Oxford University Press, 1992.

Barrett, C. K. *Church, Ministry, and Sacraments in the New Testament.* Grand Rapids: Eerdmans, 1985.

Bates, Matthew W. *Gospel Allegiance: What Faith in Jesus Misses for Salvation in Christ.* Grand Rapids: Brazos, 2019.

Bauckham, Richard. "Kingdom and Church According to Jesus and Paul." *Horizons in Biblical Theology.* 18 (1996): 1–26.

Berry, Wendell. *The Hidden Wound.* Boston: Houghton Mifflin, 1970. Repr., Berkeley: Counterpoint, 2010.

Bonhoeffer, Dietrich. *Letters and Papers from Prison.* Edited by John W. De Gruchy. Dietrich Bonhoeffer Works 8. Minneapolis: Fortress, 2010.

———. *Life Together* (1939). Translated by Daniel W. Bloesch. Edited by Geffrey B. Kelly. Dietrich Bonhoeffer Works 5. Minneapolis: Fortress, 1996.

———. *Sanctorum Communio: A Theological Study of the Sociology of the Church.* Translated by Reinhard Krauss and Nancy Lukens. Edited by Clifford J. Green. Dietrich Bonhoeffer Works 1. Minneapolis: Fortress, 1998.

Bourne, George. *The Book and Slavery Irreconcilable.* Philadelphia: Sanderson, 1816.

Bradley, Keith. *Slavery and Society at Rome.* Cambridge: Cambridge University Press, 1994.

Brill Dictionary of Ancient Greek. Leiden: Brill, 2014.

Brooks, David. "The Power of a Dinner Table." *The New York Times* (18 Oct. 2016).

Brown, Peter. *Augustine of Hippo: A Biography.* London: Faber & Faber, 1967.

Brueggemann, Walter. "Psalms and the Life of Faith: A Suggested Typology of Function." *Journal for the Study of the Old Testament* 17 (1980): 3–32, reprinted in *The Psalms and the Life of Faith.* Edited by Patrick D. Miller. Minneapolis: Fortress, 1995.

——. "Praise and the Psalms: A Politics of Glad Abandonment," *The Hymn* (October 1992), reprinted in *The Psalms and the Life of Faith.* Edited by Patrick D. Miller. Minneapolis: Fortress, 1995.

Bunting, Annie, and Joel Quirk., eds. *Contemporary Slavery: Popular Rhetoric and Political Practice.* Vancouver: UBC Press, 2017.

Burgess, Joseph A. *A History of the Exegesis of Matthew 16:17–19 from 1781 to 1965.* Ann Arbor: Edwards Brothers, 1976.

The Cambridge Greek Lexicon. Cambridge: Cambridge University Press, 2021.

Campbell, Alexander. *Familiar Lectures on the Pentateuch.* Cincinnati: Bosworth, 1867.

——. "Sermon on the Law." *Millennial Harbinger* (September 1846), 493–521.

——. "Tracts for the People—No. XXXIII. A Tract for the People of Kentucky." *Millennial Harbinger* (May 1849): 241–52.

Cone, James. *The Cross and the Lynching Tree.* Maryknoll, NY: Orbis, 2011.

Daniell, David. *William Tyndale: A Biography.* New Haven, CT: Yale University Press, 1994.

Danker, Frederick W., ed. *A Greek-English Lexicon of the New Testament and Other Early Christian Literature.* 3d ed. Chicago: University of Chicago Press, 2000.

Davies, W. D., and D. C. Allison, *The Gospel According to Saint Matthew,* 3 vols. International Critical Commentary. London: T&T Clark, 1988–97.

The Debates in the Several State Conventions, on the Adoption of the Federal Constitution, as Recommended by the General Convention at Phil-

adelphia in 1787. Edited by Jonathan Elliot. 4 vols. Washington: Printed for the Editor, 1836–1845.

Diagnostic and Statistical Manual of Mental Disorders. 5th ed. Washington, DC: American Psychiatric Publishing, 2013.

Domestic Slavery Considered as a Scriptural Institution. Edited by Nathan A. Finn and Keith Harper. Macon, GA: Mercer University Press, 2008.

Douglass, Frederick. *The Portable Frederick Douglass.* Edited by John Stauffer and Henry Louis Gates, Jr. New York: Penguin, 2016.

Downs, David J. "Economics." Pages 219–26 in *Dictionary of Jesus and the Gospels.* 2d ed. Edited by Joel B. Green. Downers Grove, IL: IVP, 2013.

Du Toit, Andrie. "Paulus Oecumenicus: Interculturality in the Shaping of Paul's Theology." *New Testament Studies* 55 (2009): 121–43.

Foster, Douglas A. *A Life of Alexander Campbell.* Grand Rapids: Eerdmans, 2020.

French, David. "You Are Only One Step Away from Complete and Total Insanity." *TheDispatch.com.* February 14, 2021.

Gallagher, Ed. "The Bible on Slavery: Approaching Ephesians 6:4–9." Pages 81–92 in *For the Glory of God: Christ and the Church in Ephesians*, Berean Study Series. Edited by Ed Gallagher. Florence, AL: Heritage Christian University Press, 2021.

———. *The Book of Exodus: Explorations in Christian Theology.* Cypress Bible Study Series. Florence, AL: Heritage Christian University Press, 2020.

———. "The Challenge of Love: Approaching Hosea." Pages 42–52 in *Visions of Grace: Stories from Scripture.* Berean Study Series. Edited by Ed Gallagher. Florence, AL: Heritage Christian University Press, 2019.

———. "Does Amos Comdemn All Sacrifice: Approaching Amos 5?" Pages 212–17 in *Proclamation and Promise: Major Themes in the Minor Prophets. The 75th Annual Freed-Hardeman University Lectureship,* Edited by David L. Lipe. Henderson, TN.: Freed-Hardeman University, 2011.

———. "God is Our Foundation: Approaching Matthew 7:24–27 // Luke 6:46–49." Pages 78–87 in *A Gentle and Quiet Spirit: A Festschrift for Barbara Ann Dillon.* Heritage Legacy Series. Edited by Staff of Heritage Christian University Press. Florence, AL: Heritage Christian University Press, 2023.

———. "The Israel of God." *Gospel Advocate* 156.3 (March 2014): 26–29.

———. "The Kingdom of God." Pages 13–21 in *The Ekklesia of Christ: Becoming the People of God.* Berean Study Series. Edited by Ed Gallagher. Florence, AL: Heritage Christian University Press, 2019.

——. "Not Under the Law: Approaching Galatians 5:18." Pages 14–22 in *Led by God's Spirit: A Practical Study of Galatians 5:22–26*, Berean Study Series. Edited by Bill Bagents. Florence, AL: Heritage Christian University Press, 2023.

——. "On Faith: Approaching Hebrews 11:1." Pages 3–12 in *Cloud of Witnesses: Ancient Stories of Faith*, Berean Study Series. Edited by Ed Gallagher. Florence, AL: Heritage Christian University Press, 2020.

——. "A Prostitute's Wish: Approaching 1 Kings 3." Pages 114–125 in *Things Most Surely Believed: Festschrift for C. Wayne Kilpatrick*. Heritage Legacy Series. Edited by Staff of Heritage Christian University Press, Florence, AL: Heritage Christian University Press, 2021.

——. *The Sermon on the Mount: Explorations in Christian Practice.* Cypress Bible Study Series. Florence, AL: Heritage Christian University Press, 2021.

——. "A Sickness Not Unto Death: Approaching John 11." Pages 115–128 in *Serving the Lord: A Festschrift for Freddie Patrick Moon and Janet Stewart Moon*. Heritage Legacy Series. Edited by Staff of Heritage Christian University. Florence, AL: Heritage Chrisitan University Press, 2022.

——. "A Still Small Voice: Approaching 1 Kings 19." Pages 88–105 in *Fighting the Good Fight: A Festschrift for Bill Bagents*. Heritage Legacy Series. Edited by Staff of Heritage Christian University Press. Florence, AL: Heritage Christian University Press, 2022.

——. "A Time for Defiance: Approaching Esther 3." Pages 119–31 *For Such a Time as This: Restoring God's People in Ezra, Nehemiah, and Esther*. Edited by Doug Burleson. Henderson, TN: FHU Press, 2023.

——. "Using Your Talents: Approaching Matthew 25:14–30." Pages 30–38 in *What Real Christianity Looks Like: A Study of the Parables*, Berean Study Series. Edited by Ed Gallagher. Florence, AL: Heritage Christian University Press, 2016.

——. "Why the Church?" Pages 3–12 in *The Ekklesia of Christ: Becoming the People of God*. Berean Study Series. Edited by Ed Gallagher. Florence, AL: Heritage Christian University Press, 2019.

——. "A Worshiping Community on a Mandated Break." *Journal of Christian Studies* 1 (2022): 9–25.

Garnsey, Peter. *Ideas of Slavery from Aristotle to Augustine.* Cambridge: Cambridge University Press, 1996.

George, Andrew. *The Epic of Gilgamesh*, 2d ed. London: Penguin, 2020.

Grafton, Thomas W. *Alexander Campbell: Leader of the Great Reformation of the Nineteenth Century.* St. Louis: Christian Publishing Company, 1897.

Gray, George Buchanan. *A Critical and Exegetical Commentary on the Book of Isaiah.* 2 vols. International Critical Commentary. Edinburgh: T&T Clark, 1912.

Greig, Pete. *How to Pray: A Simple Guide for Normal People.* Carol Stream, IL: NavPress, 2019.

Gupta, Nijay K. *Paul and the Language of Faith.* Grand Rapids: Eerdmans, 2020.

Hardeman, N. B. *Hardeman's Tabernacle Sermons.* vol. 1. 1922; repr. Henderson, TN: Freed-Hardeman University, 1990.

Harper, William. *Anniversary Oration, in the Representative Hall, Columbia, S.C., Dec. 9, 1835.* Washington: Duff Green, 1836.

Hartog, Paul. *Polycarp's Epistle to the Philippians and the Martyrdom of Polycarp: Introduction, Text, and Commentary.* Oxford: Oxford University Press, 2013.

Hays, Richard B. *Echoes of Scripture in the Letters of Paul.* New Haven: Yale University Press, 1989.

Hess, Richard S. *Israelite Religions: An Archaeological and Biblical Survey.* Grand Rapids: Baker, 2007.

Holmes, Michael W., ed., *The Apostolic Fathers: Greek Texts and English Translations.* 3d ed. Grand Rapids: Baker, 2007.

Hughes, Richard T. *Reviving the Ancient Faith: The Story of Churches of Christ in America.* Grand Rapids: Eerdmans, 1996.

Hundley, Michael. *Yahweh among the Gods: The Divine in Genesis, Exodus, and the Ancient Near East.* Cambridge: Cambridge University Press, 2022.

Hunt, Peter. *Ancient Greek and Roman Slavery.* Malden, MA: Wiley-Blackwell, 2018.

Hurtado, Larry W. *Destroyer of the Gods: Early Christian Distinctiveness in the Roman World.* Waco: Baylor University Press, 2016.

Hunter, James Davison. *To Change the World: The Irony, Tragedy, and Possibility of Christianity in the Late Modern World.* Oxford: Oxford University Press, 2010.

Huska, Liuan. "Cohousing: The New American Family." *Christianity Today* (28 Nov. 2016).

Jacobs, Harriet. *Incidents in the Life of a Slave Girl* (Boston, 1861); ed. Frances Smith Foster and Richard Yarborough. Norton Critical Edition. 2d ed. New York: Norton, 2019.

Jeremias, Jörg. *The Book of Amos: A Commentary.* Old Testament Library. Louisville: WJK, 1998.

John Paul II. *Evangelium Vitae.* 1995.

Key, Barclay. *Race and Restoration: Churches of Christ and the Black Freedom Struggle.* Baton Rouge: Louisiana State University Press, 2020.

Kidd, Thomas S. *America's Religious History: Faith, Politics, and the Shaping of a Nation.* Grand Rapids: Zondervan, 2019.

Kuhrt, Amélie. *The Persian Empire: A Corpus of Sources from the Achaemenid Period.* London: Routledge, 2007.

Lenski, Noel, and Catherine M. Cameron., eds., *What Is a Slave Society? The Practice of Slavery in Global Perspective.* Cambridge: Cambridge University Press, 2018.

Levenson, Jon D. *Resurrection and the Restoration of Israel: The Ultimate Victory of the God of Life.* New Haven, CT: Yale University Press, 2006.

Levin, Amy-Jill. *Short Stories by Jesus: The Enigmatic Parables of a Controversial Rabbi.* New York: HarperOne, 2014.

Lewis, C. S. *The Four Loves.* London: Geoffrey Bles, 1960.

———. *The Silver Chair.* The Chronicles of Narnia. New York: HarperCollins, 1953.

Lewis, Jack P. "'The Gates of Hell Shall Not Prevail Against It' (Matt 16:18): A Study of the History of Interpretation." *Journal of the Evangelical Theological Society* 38 (1995): 349–67.

Lindsay, Dennis R. "*Pistis* and *'Emunah*: The Nature of Faith in the Epistle to the Hebrews." Pages 158–69 in *A Cloud of Witnesses: The Theology of Hebrews in Its Ancient Contexts.* The Library of New Testament Studies. Edited by Richard Bauckham, Daniel Driver, Trevor Hart, Nathan MacDonald. London: T&T Clark, 2008.

Loisy, Alfred. *L'Évangile et l'Église.* 3rd ed.; Bellevue: Chez l'auteur, 1904.

Marsh, Charles. *Strange Glory: A Life of Dietrich Bonhoeffer.* New York: Knopf, 2014.

McCaulley, Esau. *Reading While Black: African American Biblical Interpretation as an Exercise in Hope.* Downers Grove, IL: IVP, 2020.

McGowan, Andrew B. *Ancient Christian Worship: Early Church Practices in Social, Historical, and Theological Perspective.* Grand Rapids: Baker, 2013.

McKnight, Scot. *Kingdom Conspiracy: Returning to the Radical Mission of the Local Church.* Grand Rapids: Brazos, 2014.

Moberly, R. W. L. *The Theology of the Book of Genesis*. Cambridge: Cambridge University Press, 2009.

Morgan, Teresa. *Roman Faith and Christian Faith*: Pistis *and* Fides *in the Early Roman Empire and Early Churches*. Oxford: Oxford University Press, 2015.

Muraoka, T. *A Greek-English Lexicon of the Septuagint*. Leuven: Peeters, 2009.

Novenson, Matthew V. *Christ among the Messiahs: Christ Language in Paul and Messiah Language in Ancient Judaism*. Oxford: Oxford University Press, 2012.

Pennington, Jonathan T. *Heaven and Earth in the Gospel of Matthew*. Leiden: Brill, 2007; Grand Rapids: Baker, 2009.

Peterson, Eugene H. *Eat This Book: A Conversation in the Art of Spiritual Reading*. Grand Rapids: Eerdmans, 2006.

Ramelli, Ilaria. *Social Justice and the Legitimacy of Slavery: The Role of Philosophical Asceticism from Ancient Judaism to Late Antiquity*. Oxford: Oxford University Press, 2016.

Richardson, Robert *Memoirs of Alexander Campbell*. 2 vols. Philadelphia: J. B. Lippincott & Co., 1868–1870.

Robinson, Edward J. *Hard-Fighting Soldiers: A History of African American Churches of Christ*. Knoxville: University of Tennessee Press, 2019.

Robinson, Marilynne. *Gilead*. New York: Farrar, Straus and Giroux, 2004.

Roth, Martha T. *Law Collections from Mesopotamia and Asia Minor*. 2d ed. Atlanta: SBL, 1997.

Schechter, Solomon. *Aspects of Rabbinic Theology: Major Concepts of the Talmud*. New York: Macmillan, 1909.

Silva, Moisés. *Biblical Words and Their Meaning: An Introduction to Lexical Semantics*. 2d ed. Grand Rapids: Zondervan, 1994.

Simonetti, Manlio., ed., *Matthew 14–28*. Ancient Christian Commentary on Scripture. Downers Grove, IL: IVP, 2002.

Smith, James K. A. *Desiring the Kingdom: Worship, Worldview, and Cultural Formation*. Grand Rapids: Baker, 2009.

Sommar, Mary E. *The Slaves of the Churches: A History*. Oxford: Oxford University Press, 2020.

Still, Todd D. "*Christos* as *Pistos*: The Faith(fulness) of Jesus in the Epistle to the Hebrews." Pages 40–50 in *A Cloud of Witnesses: The Theology of Hebrews in Its Ancient Contexts*. The Library of New Testament Studies. Edited by Richard Bauckham, Daniel Driver, Trevor Hart, Nathan MacDonald. London: T&T Clark, 2008. 40–50.

Thurman, Howard. *Jesus and the Disinherited*. Boston: Beacon, 1976.

Tisby, Jemar, and Lecrae Moore. *The Color of Compromise: The Truth about the American Church's Complicity in Racism*. Grand Rapids: Zondervan, 2019.

Trebilco, Paul. *Self-Designations and Group Identity in the New Testament*. Cambridge: Cambridge University Press, 2012.

Trueman, Carl R. *Strange New World: How Thinkers and Activists Redefined Identity and Sparked the Sexual Revolution*. Wheaton, IL: Crossway, 2022.

Turner, David L. *Matthew*, Baker Exegetical Commentary on the New Testament. Grand Rapids: Baker, 2008.

von Rad, Gerhard. *Old Testament Theology*, 2 vols. New York: Harper & Row, 1965.

West, Earl Irvin. *The Search for the Ancient Order: A History of the Restoration Movement 1849–1950*. Vol. 1. Indianapolis: Religious Book Service, 1949.

Westerholm, Stephen. *Perspectives Old and New on Paul: The "Lutheran" Paul and His Critics*. Grand Rapids: Eerdmans, 2004.

Yarhouse, Mark A. *Understanding Gender Dysphoria: Navigating Transgender Issues in a Changing Culture*. Downers Grove, IL: IVP, 2015.

Scripture Index

Old Testament

Genesis

1–11	163–164	17:11	113
1:31	163	17:12	113
2:18	186	17:12–13	113
3	164	17:14	113
3:1–7	164	22	178
3:14–19	164	22:18	147, 164
4:3–5	61	23:7	36
4:8	164	23:12	36
4:23–24	164	26:4	164
6–9	164	26:25	61
6:5	164	28:14	164
8:20	61	31:54	61
8:21	164	32:28	164
12:1–3	164	33:20	61
12:3	161, 166–167	46:1	61
12:7	61	**Exodus**	
15:6	138, 163	2:16–21	61
17:5	164	3:18	61
17:10	113	5:3	61

12:3–10	61	12:3	113
12:27	61	19:18	114, 119
12:44	113	25:39–55	125
12:48	113	**Numbers**	
13:11–15	61	20:7–11	viii
16:4	72	**Deuteronomy**	
17:6	viii	4:9–20	58
18:7	36	5:8–10	58
18:12	61	6:13	45, 74
19	24	6:16	74
19:5–6	164	8:3	71–72
19:6	167	12	58
19:16–19	23	13:5	17
20:4–6	58	15:12–18	125
20:18–19	23	23	189
20:24	62	23:15–16	134
21:1–6	125	24:7	126
21:16	126	25:4	147
22:21–27	57	27–28	164
23:18–19	62	28:58–68	165
24:5	62	31:30	149, 188
32	147	**Joshua**	
32:1–6	49	5	113
32:4	49	8:31	62
33:21–34:8	22	9	3
Leviticus		**Judges**	
1–7	62	2:5	62
1:9	198	**1 Samuel**	
2:11	58	1:3	62
8:3	149	8:7	160
10:1–2	62		

13:8–14	62	4:29–34	4
15:2–3	62	5:13–18	5
15:8	35	8:17–20	94
15:20–21	35, 62	8:25	94
15:21	62	9:20–22	5
15:22	62	11	5
15:33	35	11:1–8	155
16:1	155	11:43	104
17	94, 143	12	48
2 Samuel		12:1–15	155
7	93, 155	12:4	5, 155
7:11	94	12:26–28	58
7:12–14	94	12:26–33	49
7:12–16	155	12:28	49
7:14	155	12:28–29	57
7:15	94	12:30	58
8	94	12:31	58
1 Kings		14:20	104
		15:30	58
1–11	4	16:31	49
3	2, 4–6	17–18	59
3–10	155	18	16, 49
3:3	2, 5	18:4	22
3:4	2	18:19	17
3:5	3	18:22	22
3:9	4	18:27	17
3:10–14	4	18:36–37	17
3:17	7	18:38	17
3:17–22	6	18:39	17
3:23–25	6	18:40	17
3:26	6–7	19	14–15, 24,
3:27–28	6–7	31	

19:2	14, 17–18	50:7–15	198
19:3	14	51	60
19:3–4	32	51:16–17	60, 198
19:4	14, 31	69:30–31	198
19:4–7	31	91:11–12	74
19:8	14, 31	93:1	160
19:10	21	95:3	160
19:11–12	22	97	180
19:12	27	97:1	160, 180
19:14	21, 27	97:7–9	180
19:15–18	27	98:6	160
19:18	22, 49	99:1	160
19:19–21	28	103:14	175

2 Kings

Isaiah

8:7–15	28	1:10–15	198
9:1–10	28	1:11	60
14:23–29	49	1:13	63
14:25	48	1:16–17	63

1 Chronicles

		2:2–4	156–157
22:10	94	6:9	74
		6:9–10	178

Nehemiah

		9:7	94
13:1	189	11:1	94, 155

Esther

		11:2–5	156
3	34–35, 42	11:6–9	156
13:12–14	45	20	50
		28:7	62

Psalms

		41:8–9	165
24:3–4	63	42:6	165
40:6	60, 198	42:19	165
47:2	160	43:24	165
50:3	23		

44:18	165	**Hosea**	
49:1–6	165	1–3	59
49:6	147	1:1	59
50:4–9	165	1:2	50
52:13–53:12	165	2:5	50
56:1–8	156	2:8	51
60	156	2:14	51
61:1–2	74	2:15–17	52
Jeremiah		4:4	50
7	197	4:5	50
7:4	197	4:6	50, 63
7:5–10	197	4:9	63
7:9–11	63	4:11–14	63
7:11	197	4:12	50
7:22	62	4:15	50
23:5–6	156	6:1–3	199
25:9	197	6:4–6	199–200
25:12–15	197	6:6	63, 198, 200
31:31	151	6:9	63
Ezekiel		8:5–6	59
4	50	10:5	59
37:15–28	151, 156	11:1	viii, 52
40–48	156	11:2	53
43:5	156	11:3–4	53
47:1–12	156	11:6–7	53
Daniel		11:8–9	53
1	43	13:2	59
3	36	**Amos**	
6	35	1–2	57
9:24–27	177	1:1	49, 57, 59
		2:6–16	57

2:7	63
3:14	58
4:1	57, 63
4:2–3	57
4:4–5	58
4:10	196
5	57
5:5	57–58
5:10–15	63
5:11–12	57
5:21	182
5:21–24	58–60, 64, 198
5:24	64
5:25	62
6:7–14	57
7:9	58
7:10–17	57, 60
7:12–15	49
7:17	57
8:4–6	57

Jonah

3:4	48

Micah

3:5	62
3:11	62–64
4:1–3	156
4:6–8	156
5:2	94
6:6–8	63
7:6	74

Habakkuk

2:3–4	141
2:4	138

Zephaniah

1:12	64

Malachi

1:10	198
3:1	74

New Testament

Matthew

1:1	157
1:2–17	94
1:20	94
2:15	viii
4:1–11	70, 156, 170
4:10	45
4:23	170
4:23–25	157
5	202
5:3–12	157
5:4	130
5:9	95
5:10–12	130
5:14	147
5:17	165
5:17–48	158
5:21–30	69
5:23–24	63, 201
5:38–42	69

5:39	130	13:13	178
5:44	130	13:22	180
6:1–4	59	14:13–21	98
6:1–18	158	15:21–28	102
6:3–4	90	15:22	94
6:6	176	15:32–38	98
6:8	175	16:13–28	150
6:10	159	16:16	95
6:14–15	183	16:18	150–151, 189
6:24	180	16:21	95
6:25–34	69, 86, 136, 158	16:21–23	96
		16:22–23	95
7:1–2	8	16:24	130
7:1–14	158	18:15–17	151, 191
7:12	69, 203	18:15–18	158
7:13–14	69	18:23–25	88
7:21	158	18:23–35	182
7:21–23	203	19:21	90
7:24–27	76–77	20:1–16	87
7:28	97	20:30–31	94
8:5–13	101	21:9	94
8:11–12	157	21:15	94
9:9–13	211	21:31–32	157
9:13	198	22:34–40	119, 158, 204
9:18–26	103	22:40	186
9:27	94	22:41–46	94–95, 157
10:37	187	23:23	69, 201
11:2–6	157	24–25	86
12:7	198	24:15–16	95
12:23	94	24:19–20	95
13:2	98	24:21	95
13:10	178	24:42–44	86

24:45–51	86	5:21–43	103
25:1–13	86	5:35	106
25:14–30	85–86, 134	5:39	103
25:15	87	5:40	103
25:21	88	5:41–42	104
25:23	88	7:24–30	102
25:24–25	88	8:27–33	54
25:26	88	8:29	156
25:30	88	8:31	157
25:31–46	90, 158, 186, 204	8:34	157
26:52	157	9:31	157
27:38	92	10:29–30	187
28:18	158	10:31	157
28:19	147	10:33–34	157
Mark		10:42–45	157
		10:44	129
1:12–13	70	11:13	44
1:15	154	12:1–11	134
1:21	170	12:24	170
1:24	157	12:35–37	170
1:35	170	14:24	181
1:44	157	14:32–42	170
2:13–17	210	14:50	95
2:15–16	157	15:1–5	21
3:1	170	15:17	157
3:11–12	157	15:26	157
3:13–19	156	15:27	92
3:31–35	151, 187	**Luke**	
4:1–9	43	2:46–47	170
4:7	43	2:52	72, 170
4:19	44	3:7	81

3:16	81	9:24	75
3:17	81	10:30–35	200
3:21–22	70	10:31–32	186
4:1–13	70	10:38–42	102
4:2	70	11:20	156
4:3	70	11:28	76
4:8	45	12:32	160
4:13	74	12:53	75
4:16	170	13:16	156
4:16–21	157	14:26	187
4:18–19	74, 170	14:27	69
4:43	73	15:20	54
5:27	203	16:1–9	177
5:27–32	210	16:22	105
6:15	203	17:10	130
6:22–23	81	17:25	73
6:27	83	18:9–14	69
6:29	83	18:31–33	73
6:31	83	19:11–27	87
6:37	83	22:3	74
6:46–49	76–77	22:30	157
6:48	78	23:33	92
6:49	78, 81	23:35–37	97
7:1–10	101	23:35–38	92
7:6–8	102	23:38	97
7:27	74	23:39	92
7:36–50	157	23:41	92
8:10	74	23:42	92
8:40–56	103	23:43	92
9:10–17	71	24:21–24	96
9:22	73	24:27	75, 170
9:23	69, 172	24:44–45	75

John

1:1–4	109
3:3	158
4:1–2	98
5:24	105–106
5:25	109
5:26	109
6:15	157
6:60	98
7:19	116
8:51	106
10:10	109
10:34	114
11	100, 102, 108
11:3	101–102
11:4	101
11:5–6	103
11:11	103
11:14	103
11:21	101, 109
11:25	109
11:32	101, 109
11:37	109
12:24	109
12:31	73
13:1–10	157
13:3–4	129
13:15	129, 186
14:15	83
15:19	208
15:25	114
16:20	110
17:13–19	208
17:16	190
18:10	95
18:36	95
19:25–26	96–97

Acts

7	104
7:38	187–188, 207
7:60	104
9:16	55
10:25–26	36
16:19–25	21
19:32	188
19:39	188
19:40	149, 188

Romans

1:17	141
2:13	115
2:14–15	120
2:25–29	114, 120, 163
3:10–20	116
5:12	164
6:14	119
6:14–15	116
6:15	119
7:12	117
7:21	120
8	119
8:4	118
8:15–17	187

8:17	159	10:11	147
8:28	28	10:14–22	117
9:6	162	10:17	29
9:26	177	11	203
11:3	22	11:17–34	181
11:4	22	11:18	189
12:2	44, 181, 190	11:20	148, 206
12:3	85	11:24	181
12:4–5	29	11:25	181
12:6	85, 87	11:26	181
13:8–10	118	11:27	182
14:5–6	116	11:28	182
14:14	116	11:29	182
15:4	117, 147	12	203
16:1	189	12–14	85
16:5	195	12:13	128

1 Corinthians

		12:26	146–147
1:2	195	12:27	182
1:23	73, 130	14:19	189
5:1–13	117	14:21	114
6:9	159	14:28	189
6:12–20	117	14:34	117, 189
6:15	29	14:35	189
7:19	114	15:20–22	164
7:21	127	15:50	159
7:21–22	127–128	15:51	104
9:9	117		

2 Corinthians

9:9–10	147	10:5	174
9:20	116	11:24–29	55
10:1–14	117		

Galatians

10:4	viii	2:14	162

2:16	115	5:18	113–114, 116
2:21	115	5:22–23	119
3:3	114	6:2	203, 208
3:6–7	163	6:11	162
3:7	166	6:12–14	162
3:8	164	6:13	114–115
3:10	114	6:15	114
3:11	115, 141	6:15–16	162
3:13	165	6:16	162
3:14	165–166	**Ephesians**	
3:16	147	1:3	85
3:19	116	1:4	147
3:23	116	1:22	208
3:24–25	116	1:23	29
3:26–27	165	2	203
3:28	128, 130	2:8–9	83
3:29	113, 147	2:16	29
4:1	116	2:20	86, 150
4:4–5	116	3:10	147, 208
4:5–6	187	3:21	208
4:6	114	4:4	29
4:21	116	4:11–16	29, 85
4:21–31	116	4:12–16	195
4:23	114	5:1–2	56
4:29	114	5:21	130
5	119	5:23	29
5:1	116	5:23–32	208
5:2	113	5:30	29
5:4	113, 116	6	123, 129
5:6	114	6:1–3	117
5:14	114, 118	6:4–9	122, 178
5:16–17	114		

6:5	122–123, 131
6:5–9	134
6:5–8	129
6:9	127, 129

Philippians

1:21	21
2:3	203
2:6–7	129
2:9–11	159
3:20	168
4:13	21

Colossians

1:13	158
1:18	29, 147, 208
1:24	208
2:15	158
2:19	29
3:5	180
3:11	128
3:15	29
3:22–4:1	134
4:1	127
4:15	208
4:16	208

1 Thessalonians

4:3–8	117
4:11–12	227
4:15	104

1 Timothy

1:10	126

1:15	13
5:18	117
6:1–2	134

2 Timothy

2:15	117
3:16	69, 83
3:16–17	117

Titus

2:9–10	134

Hebrews

2:14–15	158
2:14–17	12
2:17	138
3:2	138
3:5	138
4:2	144
4:3	138
4:12	67, 69
4:15	67
5:7	100
5:8	72
6:1	144
6:12	144
9:16	93
10:5–7	60
10:22	144
10:23	138
10:32	141
10:33–34	141
10:36	141
10:38	138, 144

10:39	142, 144
11	137–138, 141– 143
11:1	136, 139–140
11:6	138, 140
11:11	138
11:13	142
11:16	168
11:30	143
11:32	143
12:2	141–142, 144
13:7	144

James

1:6	107
1:17	85
1:22–25	81
1:27	64
2:19	84
4:17	89

1 Peter

2:9	147, 167
2:18–21	134
3:4	227
3:15	227
4:10	85, 87

2 Peter

1:3	21

1 John

4:18	21

Revelation

1:6	160
1:10	148, 206
2:10	39, 45
4	173
5:13	159
12	173
13	173
13:4	173
13:12	173
13:16–18	173
17	173

Wisdom of Solomon

3:1	105

Didache

7.3	191

Credits

Scripture quotations marked HCSB are been taken from the Holman Christian Standard Bible®, Copyright © 1999, 2000, 2002, 2003 by Holman Bible Publishers. Used by permission. Holman Christian Standard Bible®, Holman CSB®, and HCSB® are federally registered trademarks of Holman Bible Publishers.

Scripture quotations are from the ESV® Bible (The Holy Bible, English Standard Version®), copyright © 2001 by Crossway, a publishing ministry of Good News Publishers. Used by permission. All rights reserved.

Select Scripture quotations are taken from the NEW AMERICAN STANDARD BIBLE®, copyright© 1960, 1962, 1963, 1968, 1971, 1972, 1973, 1975, 1977, 1995 by The Lockman Foundation. Used by permission.

Select Scripture quotations are taken from the NEW REVISED STANDARD VERSION BIBLE, copyright ©

Also by Ed Gallagher

Hebrew Scripture in Patristic Biblical Theory (Brill, 2012)

The Biblical Canon Lists from Early Christianity (Oxford, 2017) with John D. Meade

The Book of Exodus: Exploration in Christian Theology (Heritage Christian University Press, 2019)

The Sermon on the Mount: Exploration in Christian Practice (Heritage Christian University Press, 2020)

The Gospel of Luke: Exploration in Christian Scripture (Heritage Christian University Press, 2021)

Gallagher, Edmon L. *The Translation of the Seventy: History, Reception, and Contemporary Use of the Septuagint* (Abilene Christian University Press, 2021)

The Christian Life: Chapters for Bible Teachers (Cypress Publications, 2022)

Jesus the Christ: Chapters for Bible Teachers (Cypress Publications, 2022)

Berean Study Series edited by Ed Gallagher

(HCU Press)

HERITAGE
CHRISTIAN UNIVERSITY
PRESS

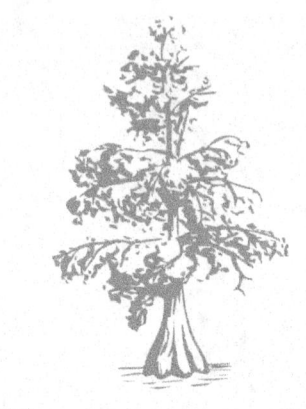

CYPRESS

To see full catalog of Heritage Christian University Press
and its imprint Cypress Publications, visit
www.hcu.edu/publications

www.ingramcontent.com/pod-product-compliance
Lightning Source LLC
Chambersburg PA
CBHW061141120626
46546CB00005B/1883